25 SUPERSONIC YEARS

CELEBRATING CONCORDE

25 SUPERSONIC YEARS

CELEBRATING CONCORDE

REGINALD TURNILL

Introduction by John W. R. Taylor

IAN ALLAN
Publishing

Dedication

This history of the Concorde project celebrates the 25th anniversary of the first flight of the world's first and only supersonic passenger airliner, and considers what comes after Concorde.

It is based upon the author's personal experiences, mainly during his career as BBC Aerospace and Defence Correspondent.

The story has been extracted from his unfinished autobiography, sub-titled 'A Reporter's Voyage Through the 20th Century', and stands alone here as a separate story.

While no disrespect is intended to those omitted, it is dedicated to some of those men (there were few if any women) whom the author encountered and admired, laughed and quarrelled with over a period of more than 30 years:

John Cochrane
Sir George Edwards
Charles Gardner
Sir Stanley Hooker
Sir Archibald Russell
Brian Trubshaw
Andre Turcat, Pierre Young
Henri Ziegler.

Front cover photograph by Allan Burney

First published 1994

ISBN 0 7110 2296 8

Designed by Ian Allan Studio

Published by Ian Allan Publishing
an imprint of Ian Allan Ltd, Terminal House, Station Approach, Shepperton, Surrey TW17 8AS; and printed by Ian Allan Printing Ltd Coombelands House, Coombelands Lane, Addlestone, Weybridge, Surrey KT15 1HY.

Contents

Acknowledgements

Grateful thanks are due to the many people who have helped in the final stages of writing and illustrating with relevant pictures this story of how Concorde survived.

British Airways' help included a transatlantic flight aboard Concorde to Washington, and back from New York, to enable me to experience Concorde's current routine operations — and my thanks are due to Tony Cocklin, BA's Head of Communications, for giving permission for it. BA's Concorde pilots who have helped included Captains John Hutchings, Dave Leney, Colin Morris, and Geoffrey Mussett. The Public Affairs staff, including Ken White, who helped to organise the famous inaugural flights, have topped me up with information and pictures. So have British Aerospace, including Robert Gardner, Howard Berry, Trevor Mason and Nick Berry. Boeing pictures have been provided by Dick Kenny and Peter Middleton. Jack de Coninck and Norman Pealing, whose film of the inaugural flights for BAC provides the permanent record of those occasions, also took many still photographs which they have generously loaned to help to tell my story. Brian Kervell, retiring Curator and Archivist of RAE Farnborough (whose records and museum are now incredibly being broken up, dispersed and destroyed) did some last-minute research for me. Mike Ramsden of Flight International and Aerospace filled in some major pictorial gaps with personal pictures of the Boeing 7207 and of Concorde and the Tu-144 at the Paris Air Show.

Graham Turnill has done much work turning mementoes, charts and old newspaper cuttings into suitable illustrations and Margaret Turnill has battled with administrative problems.

Books which I have used to check facts and dates and to fill gaps in my own knowledge, and which are invaluable for the Concorde student include:

Britain's Aircraft Industry; Arthur Reed, J. M. Dent & Sons Ltd 1973.
British Aircraft Corporation; Charles Gardner, Batsford 1981.
Concorde: The Inside Story; Geoffrey Knight, Weidenfeld & Nicolson 1976.
Concorde: The International Race for Supersonic Passenger Transport; John
    Costello and Terry Hughes, Angus & Robertson 1976.
Concorde: New shape in the Sky; Kenneth Owen, Jane's 1982.
Faster than Sound; Bill Gunston, Patrick Stephens Ltd 1992.
From the Flightdeck — Concorde; Dave Leney & Allan Burney, Ian Allan
    Publishing 1990.

Introduction

By Dr John W. R. Taylor obe, Editor Emeritus,
Jane's All the World's Aircraft.

Concorde is an immaculate subject. It is so beautiful, and, whatever they might say, most British people are so proud of it that after more than 20 years, they still look up admiringly whenever it flies overhead.

It is one of the few aeroplanes in history that has done everything it was designed to do — carrying up to 100 passengers in armchair luxury non-stop over the Atlantic between Europe and North America at twice the speed of sound, as a daily routine throughout the year, *in perfect safety*. It has never hurt a passenger in all its yeasr of service.

It is an achievement of which Britain and France can be proud. We have taken passengers into the supersonic age, pointing the way to an inevitable future. The Russians tried it with the Tu-144, and failed. The Americans spent 50% as much on trying to design, and not even building, a supersonic transport as we spent on building 16 Concordes.

Reg Turnill, as BBC Air Correspondent, grew up with Concorde, from its first concept (as the French Super Caravelle) to its entry into service. He traced its every problem; knew and interviewed those who promoted and designed Concorde and those who sought to prevent its ever going into service. Nobody could write a better in-depth analysis of the whole story, telling it from personal experience, and in the words of those most involved. He is not prejudiced at any stage, telling of the problems associated with supersonic flight as clearly as its unrivalled attractions.

He pulls no punches in retelling (as once broadcast) the difficulties experienced in working with the very nationalistic French, who always tried to emphasise themselves as the No.1 partner, which they were not. Equally he makes clear that it was French determination that kept the programme alive in its gloomiest days. He is not afraid to mention the obstruction he encountered as the result of his predecessor as BBC Air Correspondent being in charge of BAC's Concorde press relations. He gives a true picture of how Freddie Laker emerged briefly as Concorde's saviour when BOAC became weak-kneed (as they had been most of the time).

America's sulky obstructionism, and attempt to use Concorde as a stepping-stone to their own, potentially enormously profitable, larger, faster supersonic transport, is explained dispassionately.

The true facts of the Tu-144 'Concordski' crash at the Paris Air Show are explained in simple terms. This puts right much previous inaccurate reporting and innuendo. It reflects his long experience in reporting truth, simply and in as few words as possible, on TV and radio.

7

The book must be accurate, because the author is able to refer to recorded interviews, copious records, and carefully-preserved memorabilia associated with every phase of the story.

This includes salutory observations on the worth of luxurious free meals and giveaways to the kind of people who can afford to travel on Concorde today. They should be heeded by all airline operators.

This is a story that *had* to be told, to ensure that future generations get it right. It is also extremely readable.

Author's Note:

The success of the Anglo-French supersonic airliner is one of the major achievements of the 20th century.

It was fitting that Concorde first flew in 1969, paralleling the United States' achievement in landing the first men on the moon.

Anyone tempted to argue that the moonlanding was the greater of the two technological advances would do well to remember that Project Apollo was carried through in an atmosphere of almost universal support and encouragement. Those involved in Project Concorde had to persist against a background of repeated political attempts to cancel it, and — in retrospect — an astonishing campaign of journalistic lies and misrepresentation.

CHAPTER ONE

The First 21 Years

The Concorde story began for me at the Paris Air Show in June 1961, and for 15 years afterwards involved me in personal controversy and acrimony until the story ended with a measure of happiness with coverage of the inaugural flights in 1976. It started with an interview about a proposed 'Super Caravelle' in a 25-minute BBC programme called 'TV News Extra'. The name Concord(e), with all its ironic undertones, was still several years away from its invention by the son of a Bristol public relations officer.

The US Air Force had set the supersonic theme for the Air Show by making the first faster-than-sound transatlantic crossing with one of their new Convair Hustler bombers — New York to Paris in 3hr 19min at a speed of 1,105mph. A somewhat unrewarding interviewee, the commander, Major William Payne, told me: 'I'd say the major difference is that it's faster. Other than that, it's just like sitting at home in the rocking chair.' (Eight days later, however, the same Hustler, flown by a different three-man crew, crashed during the Air Show, killing them all.)

Many years later, when writing *Farnborough: The Story of RAE*, I was to learn from Sir Morien Morgan how the British Government decided to go ahead with development of an experimental supersonic aircraft in 1943 — a year before the first jet fighter flew. In the best British tradition, the programme was cancelled in 1946 a few months before the first of three Miles Aircraft prototypes was ready to fly. Morgan said he was relieved at the cancellation, for he was convinced they would fail — but their straight-wing configuration was remarkably similar to the US aircraft in which Chuck Yeager went through the sound barrier before Britain achieved it.

By the early 1950s, America had four supersonic military projects under way, while in the words of Arnold Hall, who at 36 had become the youngest-ever Director of RAE, Britain was 'still dithering around' with models, designs and experimental aircraft. Some of the 'dithering' however did prove useful, because it included the launching of sharp-edged, delta-wing models looking much like the future Concorde, from the bedroom window of an RAE scientist named W. E. Gray.

That at least proved that the right-angle wings thought to be essential to support the aircraft for landing at relatively low speeds could be dispensed with in favour of the swept wings required for high speed flight.

A discussion paper dated April 1955, led by Morien Morgan, was followed by the setting up in November 1956 of the Supersonic Transport Aircraft Committee with Morgan as chairman. It included representatives of nine aircraft and four engine makers, the national airlines and Government officials. Little had been heard of their work, which they all regarded as terribly secret as well as terribly important. (They were however invariably willing to share it with their opposite numbers in other countries, including Germany right up to the start of World War Two, but not with the public!) By March 1959, however, the Committee had got around to recommending that two supersonic passenger aircraft should be built — a long-range version carrying 150 passengers at Mach 1.8 (1,200mph); and a shorter-range aircraft carrying 100 passengers cruising at Mach 1.2 (800mph). The Committee was worried about ground noise — they expected that 8-12 engines would be needed, and thought that 'sonic bang may cause some alarm until the populace gets used to it'. In-service dates were targeted for 1968/69 for the smaller aircraft, with the bigger version a year later.

All these documents were still stamped 'secret' when I was writing my Farnborough book 15 years later. ('Our policy is to classify everything, then everyone knows where they stand.') No one was ever given the task of declassifying anything; so Brian Kervell, of RAE's Library, solved the problem for me by using a paper guillotine to cut off the tops of the pages bearing the classification.

The secrecy of course largely explained why I knew nothing of these very tentative plans when in 1961 I interviewed M. Georges Hereilt, head of Sud Aviation — one of many companies now merged into France's Aerospatiale consortium. While Britain was sorting out its Comet problems, Sud had swept ahead with the Caravelle, powered by the same Rolls Royce jet engines, and was very angry that Britain's national airlines had not bought any. Now M. Hereilt stood beaming behind a large model of the proposed supersonic 'Super Caravelle', while I reached across it to hold my cup-shaped BBC microphone under his nose. He expressed the hope that the Super Caravelle would have British engines — for the simple reason that the French still had a long way to go before catching up on jet technology. (When the time came they were in fact Bristol Siddeley Olympus jets, originally developed for the second generation Vulcan V-bombers; at the end of the century Concorde was still powered by these engines designed 40 years earlier!) The routes for the Super Caravelle, said Hereilt, would be London-Cairo, London-Beirut, London-Athens, and coast-to-coast in the US: New York-Los Angeles and New York-San Francisco.

'This is a big surprise,' I said. 'We've been taught for years that no supersonic airliner can fly across land without smashing all the greenhouses!'

'We know that, but we have quite a lot of experience — secret experience — and we know it is a problem, but not too big. We know these problems, and even if big, we can solve them.'

I pushed harder and M. Hereilt claimed to be 'sure' that Sud could overcome the supersonic bang. Cedric Turner, head of Australia's national airline, Qantas, was so impressed that in 1960 he flew round the world visiting the US, Britain, France and the Soviet Union to study what they were doing about supersonics. He then told me that he would be requiring four or five aircraft — even though they were estimated to cost a prohibitive £5 million each — and actually issued a supersonic timetable. This gave a 10am take-off time from Sydney, arriving in London 10 hours later at 1.45pm in time for a late lunch.

10

When success seemed certain: Stewardesses from 15 of the 16 'Concorde airlines' parade with Concorde prototype 002 at Farnborough. *de Coninck*

France's proposed supersonic aircraft, displayed at the 1961 Paris Air Show. M Georges Hereilt head of Sud Aviation (later merged into Aerospatiale) explains its potential to the author. *Sud Aviation*

Turner also outlined his specifications: 2,000mph, cruising at 70,000ft — the same height as America's U2 spy plane, one of which the Soviets had just shot down. The aircraft would be torpedo-shaped, with delta wings at the rear, with TV screens instead of windows for the 90 passengers — and the flight would be completely automated. Turner however was out of step with the big airlines like Pan American, TWA and BOAC. They were committed to spending large sums on fleets of subsonic jets, and were agreed upon one thing — they wanted the supersonic age delayed as long as possible, and that meant for at least 10 years.

In the autumn that year there were some discussions on international supersonic collaboration during Aviation Minister Peter Thorneycroft's more pressing talks on space collaboration. The Americans made it clear they could manage very well on their own, but the French were at that time much more interested in supersonic aircraft than joining in the space race.

Five hundred aviation experts from Britain, the US and Canada gathered in London in September 1961 to consider how fast a supersonic aircraft ought to fly. Dr Archie Russell (later Sir Archibald), favoured Mach 2, or twice the speed of sound (1,320mph) and said that that would cost the passengers £4 per hour extra for each hour of saved time. The Americans favoured Mach 3 (1,980mph), which Russell estimated would cost £16 per hour for four hours of saved time.

The US Federal Aviation Administration, which was working on the basis that there would be 200 supersonic aircraft operating by the mid-1970s (when that time came it was nine Concordes), insisted that there must be windows, citing the fact that Alan Shepard, first American in space, had demanded a bigger window in the Mercury spacecraft. Other FAA predictions proved to be wildly wrong: they forecast that by the mid-1970s only economy passengers would be using the supersonic planes, because all the first-class passengers would be flying around in their own private jets.

'There might, however, be a requirement for a small, exclusive section for film stars.' Currently — in early 1994 — it seems certain that no economy class passengers will ever fly in Concorde, and that supersonics will alas be used exclusively by the rich until well into the 21st century.

That September 1961 conference, bringing out into the open differing views, and especially US views, on what sort of animal the first SST should be, marked a decision point. Shortly afterwards the British Aircraft Corporation completed a £350,000 feasibility study on the subject, and the conclusions proposed an aircraft very similar to Sud Aviation's Super Caravelle. 'To spread the development costs — perhaps £50 to £100 millions', I broadcast, 'and make sure of plenty of customers on the Continent, it seems sensible for BAC and Sud Aviation to work together. The engines are likely to be British anyway, and on this basis the French might well argue that they should take the lead with the airframe.'

By March 1962, the two countries had agreed at both Government and industry level on the preliminary design — a narrow-delta jetliner, flying at Mach 2.2, or 1500 mph, and that long-range and medium range versions would be built respectively by Britain and France. Both development costs 'and profit, if any' would be pooled. It was at this time that the US made a rare mistake in the aviation business — a decision to build a more advanced supersonic transport capable of Mach 3.

13

Sir Aubrey Burke, of de Havilland, by then part of Hawker Siddeley, told the International Air Transport Association in September 1962 that the Anglo-French decision to develop an SST was 'lunacy', and that the money would be better used for safety systems like automatic landing. Happily for the rest of the aircraft industry his views were ignored, and on 29 November 1962 Aviation Minister Julian Amery and Geoffrey de Courcel, the French Ambassador in London, signed the Anglo-French Supersonic Treaty. It was apparently Amery who had deliberately made it a Treaty without a break clause to ensure that the French could not withdraw from it (as they had withdrawn from other joint aircraft projects) without becoming liable to heavy penalties. Without such a Treaty the project would never have survived; only two years later, as described later, it worked the other way round when Britain's new Labour Government was angrily thwarted in an attempt to kill it. After the signature Amery told the House of Commons that without the project Britain would have to abandon its position as a leading aviation country; with it there was every chance that Britain and France would secure a substantial part of the world market for 200-300 supersonic aircraft.

The small print of the agreement made it all look most unpromising: The UK was to 'lead' on the Olympus engine, and in return France's nationalised engine company, SNECMA, was to be responsible for the engine nozzles. Because the engine was so important (usually considered to represent about 30% of the project). France was to 'lead' on the airframe, and have 60% of the work; but the British Aircraft Corporation was to be responsible for the nose and its 'droop-snoot', the forward and rear fuselage, the fin, rudder and nacelles, including the air intakes and the engine bays.

That left the French the wings, centre section, elevons and undercarriage. The media were soon producing blue and red colour charts to make sense of that for the public.

Archie Russell, who was right in predicting that the US planemakers were planning the impossible, got it wrong for once in a Radio News Reel interview in which he forecast a maximum production rate of 18 aircraft per year in each country — 36 Concordes a year!

The rows about the project started immediately — but about the name, rather than the engineering split which worked reasonably well from the start. A young Cambridge undergraduate, Tim Clark, who was the son of BAC's Filton publicity manager, suggested the name Concord(e), which was passed up to Sir George Edwards.

He liked it and thought that inclusion of the final 'e' would look more attractive on the fuselage and would also please his opposite number, General Andre Puget of Sud Aviation. The General was pleased, and his company expressed their pleasure by giving young Clark a week's 'all found' holiday in Paris. He spent one hour at the Paris Air Show to receive an award and the remainder in the picture galleries — for Clark was on his way to becoming Professor of the History of Art at an American university. Unlike the General, Julian Amery was most displeased because neither he nor the British Government, funding the project, had been consulted. But Peter (now Lord) Thorneycroft, Amery's immediate predecessor as Aviation Minister, had equally not bothered to inform George Edwards (as Sir George confirmed to me in early 1993) that he had been discussing with the French Government 'Alliance' and 'Europa' as possible names.

14

Above: **The men who steered Concorde through the political maze: Left, Sir George Edwards, Chairman, British Aircraft Corporation; and right, General Henri Ziegler, President of Aerospatiale, as Sud Aviation later became.**

Below: **An artist's impression of a Concorde taxying at Heathrow during one of BOAC's early enthusiastic periods.** *BOAC*

When de Gaulle almost at the same time refused British entry to the European Common Market, BAC was ordered to drop the final 'e' — which promptly became known at Filton as 'the French letter'.

George Edwards, having agreed on the name with Puget, refused to do so, and for the next five years all BAC press releases spelt the name 'Concorde', while the equally prolific Government handouts used 'Concord'!

Five months after the Anglo-French agreement had been signed, the worries started over the sonic bang. M. Hereilt's assertion that the French had a secret solution to the problem was disproved by tests carried out by British Lightning and French Mirage aircraft in Europe and compared with similar tests conducted in the US. Just how far the public had been misled by M. Hereilt became clear at a 'non-attributable briefing' which I was given in January 1963 on a visit to Bristol Siddeley Engines — still sturdily independent, with the take-over by Rolls-Royce three years away.

A technical report headed 'Sonic Boom Overpressure Problems' provided by Dr Archie Russell described how measurements had shown that the pressure wave caused by an aircraft flying faster than the speed of sound not only hit a person's ear when it rebounded from the ground; if the person was standing near a wall the simultaneous rebound from that could have a most unpleasant focusing effect. An overpressure of two pounds could be 'pretty horrid', Russell told me — and sonic bangs could rise to eight times the normal air pressure. A measure of the difficulty of the problem was that the boom could vary as much as 20-50% between morning and afternoon; the boom could be sharpest in a still atmosphere, likely to occur in the early morning. America's proposal for an SST weighing 400,000lb and flying at Mach 3 was not possible, added Russell, because its sonic boom would be unacceptable unless it flew at 80,000ft, and at that height the dangers of solar radiation would be too great. (I assumed at the time that this could be largely discounted as forgivable 'knocking' of the opposition, but learned later that 'Doc Russells' maths were always right!)

However, scientists in Britain, France and the US had all concluded that supersonic aircraft must not be allowed to cause overpressures of more than three-quarters of a pound, so that even when they were doubled by focusing, the human ear, to say nothing of plaster ceilings, would not be subjected to more than 1.5 pounds. All this affected Concorde design, since the aircraft's weight and altitude were major factors in causing the overpressure. Concorde must thus be lighter than a Boeing 707 and given a 'needle-nose' because that made less of a 'whipcrack'; it must not pass over cities at supersonic speeds, nor go through the sound barrier at altitudes of less than 35,000ft. Fortunately for Europe, the US companies, like M Hereilt, thought there was no problem they could not beat, and pressed on with projects that in the end had to be abandoned.

The enthusiasm with which the supersonic sales campaign was being conducted was not therefore affected by such reports. The major airlines were not being invited to 'order' the plane, but to reserve 'options' and delivery positions. Sales teams pointed out that airlines like Pan American and TWA could not afford *not* to have SSTs when BOAC and Air France started operating them. Returning from a visit to Australia I described how successful the US sales teams had been at 'underselling' Britain's subsonic jet aircraft as well as the

Sept 1961: Peter Thorneycroft, then Minister of Aviation, looks sceptical during a BBC interview with the author at the Farnborough Air Show. *de Havilland*

Anglo-French SST. 'I've been astonished to find even airline presidents have swallowed American salesmen's stories that the Anglo-French plane has already run into difficulties, and that America's rival plane will be sooner and faster,' I reported. 'When you gently point out that America hasn't even decided what sort of supersonic plane to build, let alone started manufacture, they reply darkly: "I gather there's a great deal of work going on."'

It was in fact the British who had a great deal of work going on. There were soon three research aircraft investigating potential problems within 'the supersonic envelope': two were involved with high speeds — the stainless steel Bristol T188, and the BAC 221, which was a rebuilt version of the Fairey Delta 2 which introduced the 'droop snoot' concept and had set up a world air speed record of 1,132mph in 1956; while the Handley Page 115, a slender delta vehicle, was doing research into the behaviour of such shapes at low speeds, and particularly when landing. Problems encountered with the T188 led George Edwards to the conclusion that the earlier decision to build Concorde in light alloy was the right one.

In June 1963 Pan American became the first airline to give what Najeeb Halaby, head of America's Federal Aviation Administration, dismissed as 'a kind of order' for six Concordes. It ensured they would get their first supersonic aircraft at the same time as the British and French airlines. The 'order' did not specify details of the aircraft, nor the price and delivery dates; but it did specify that three Concordes were to be supplied from France, and three from Britain, and down payments were made — nearly FFr3m to Sud Aviation, and £210,000 to BAC. By the end of that year there were 25 such options, and they peaked at 74 from 16 airlines in 1967.

Determined to have their own matching list of supersonic options, even though no decision had been made as to whether Boeing, Lockheed or North American (later Rockwell) should be given the Government contract to build it, the Federal Aviation Administration decided that they too would collect deposits against future delivery positions. US airlines, always far more nationally-oriented than Britain's, made it a point of honour when they took out Concorde options to reserve at least an equal number of mythical US supersonic options. Cedric Turner of Qantas took up options for both on the grounds that they were likely to be different sorts of aircraft, and Australia would probably wish to be operating both at the same time; but he complained bitterly that while his deposit of £400,000 for six US SSTs was returnable with interest if cancelled before 1965, not only was his £270,000 deposit on four Concordes not returnable, but there was a penalty of another £270,000 if the options were later cancelled. BOAC and Air France, who would of course get the first available Concordes, also took out two-way insurance in the form of US options and paid their deposits. Their contracts entitled BOAC to have delivery of the 17th US SST to be built, with Air France getting the 35th — with both airlines receiving their full quota of six aircraft at about the same time.

While all this was going on in the early months of 1964, the British were shocked and the French smug when Sir George Edwards disclosed in a routine lecture to the Institute of Transport that the first Concorde prototype would be completed by France in 1967 and flown by them for six months before Britain had the second in the air. At that time airline deliveries were due to start in

1971. George Edwards was a master at slipping out unpalatable aspects of the Concorde partnership on occasions like this when they might attract the least attention — but this was a story I did not miss.

Two weeks later I began a four-minute piece in 'From Our Own Correspondent' in this way: 'A lady in Oklahoma has just complained that her bra-strap broke eight times in one day. The cause of this repeated let down, she alleged, was the eight sonic booms which Oklahoma is having to endure every day for six months.' That city of 750,000 had been selected, with the approval of its Mayor and the local newspapers, for practical tests of what life might be like for those on the ground in the 'supersonic seventies'. In fact the overpressures to which Oklahoma's residents were subjected were very light, since they were caused by a tiny F104 fighter flying supersonically at over 30,000ft. After one month 4,000 people had accepted the invitation to complain, and 75 had filed claims for damages — one of them a woman who alleged that the overpressures had caused her furniture to shrink. A noticeable feature of this experiment, which also occurred when similar tests were made in Britain, was that even when bad weather caused the tests to be cancelled, the same number of complaints still came in.

Shortly after that, in May 1964, the 93 airline-members of the International Air Transport Association were told at a private briefing in Beirut that the medium-range version of Concorde had been abandoned and the one version which both Britain and France would now produce would be larger — even though it was admitted that this would increase the sonic bang. But the redesign of airframe and engine would enable it to carry 118 passengers and add 300 miles to its range, taking it over 4,000. Concorde's range, adequate for London-New York and Paris-New York, but never really comfortable for the slightly longer flight to Washington, was to be a subject of major future debate.

The extra development costs flowing from this redesign were kept quiet for another two months, when Julian Amery revealed that they had 'doubled' to £150-180 millions, to be shared between Britain and France, and that each Concorde would cost the airlines about £5 millions. But that did not look so bad against an estimated £12 millions for the US SST. There were signs of behind-the-scenes panic when the Council of Europe Economic Committee at Strasbourg proposed that 19 European airlines should pool their routes and traffic rights, lease blocks of seats to one another, and feed passengers subsonically to a small number of 'international gateways' where they would transfer to their intercontinental supersonic flights.

These proposals were forgotten for ever in the international uproar which broke out over the whole Concorde project within 10 days of Harold Wilson's Labour Government coming to power on 16 October 1964. Julian Amery was replaced as Minister of Aviation by Roy Jenkins. He was a man of erudition who knew little about aviation, appeared rather shocked that Wilson had selected him for the post, and confessed to the air correspondence that he had been 'handed the poisoned chalice'. Aviation chiefs were well aware that the new Labour administration had little love for them, and had expected to suffer some losses — possibly cancellation of the TSR2 intended to replace the V-bombers. But they certainly did not expect that the first act of the Wilson Government would be a frontal attack on Concorde. Nor did I expect that what became known as 'the Brown paper' — in fact a White Paper on the economic situation issued by

The Economic Situation

A Statement

by

Her Majesty's Government

26th October, 1964

(5) The Government will foster more rapid development in the under-employed areas of the country.

(6) The Government will carry out a strict review of all Government expenditure. Their object will be to relieve the strain on the balance of payments and release resources for more productive purposes by cutting out expenditure on items of low economic priority, such as " prestige projects ". The Government have already communicated to the French Government their wish to re-examine urgently the Concord project.

(7) The social programmes of the Government will be unfolded in the Queen's Speech. The country realises that these will have to be paid

LONDON
HER MAJESTY'S STATIONERY OFFICE
NINEPENCE NET

October 1964: The Wilson Government's 'Brown Paper' which tried to kill Concorde.

George Brown as Minister of Economic Affairs — would fall to the Air and Defence Correspondent to cover.

Paragraph 13 (6) of this eight-page document, the first official utterance to the British public by Labour after 13 years in opposition, read as follows:

'The Government will carry out a strict review of all Government expenditure. Their object will be to relieve the strain on the balance of payments and release resources for more productive purposes by cutting out expenditure on items of low economic priority, such as "prestige projects". The Government have already communicated to the French Government their wish to re-examine urgently the Concorde project.'

This was issued on a Monday, and the final sentence had apparently been added at the last moment as a result of George Brown's Permanent Under Secretary visiting Washington the previous week to negotiate a US loan of £900 million. He had taken a draft of the White Paper with him, containing no direct reference to Concorde; but the American administration, which had repeatedly urged Britain to cancel the project, had now made it a condition of the loan that Concorde should go, so that sentence was hurriedly inserted. It was not even accurate, since Britain's ambassador in Paris, summoned back from a Sunday shooting party, had been unable to make contact with the French Foreign Minister to warn him of Britain's intention to kill the Concorde.

The luckless Roy Jenkins, bearing his poisoned chalice, was despatched to Paris to sort things out, and with a TV crew I was among his pursuers. We were graciously allowed to hang about in the spacious marble entrance hall of the British Embassy. As usual the air correspondents knew in far greater detail than the Minister what was going on, as a result of unofficial briefings from both British and French aerospace executives. It was already clear that the Anglo-French Concorde agreement, negotiated by Julian Amery with no break clause so that the French could not back out, now trapped Britain. If the Wilson Government pulled out of Concorde, France could seek a ruling from the International Court at The Hague that Britain must still pay her share of the production costs with no right to any share in the benefits at the end. Added to that was the wrath of the trade unions, British and French, at the prospect of thousands of highly-skilled technicians being thrown out of work as a result of the first act of a Labour Government.

Having talked to three French ministers, Jenkins rushed back to London to report to the Government and we followed in the same aircraft, finally cornering him at London Airport. There he demonstrated a politicians' flair for evading the main issue. The French had listened 'with interest, and I think to some extent with sympathy' to Britains' urgent need, arising out of the economic situation, to review whether Concorde was a good economic proposition.

'Some reports say you went to Paris to save the Concorde project, and some say you went to bury it,' I said.

'I don't think either is true. I certainly didn't go to bury it. You can't bury something until it is dead — at least it is not very proper to bury it until it's dead — and I have said it can't be dead until a decision is announced. I went to explain why we wanted an urgent review, and I wanted to get — and we hoped to get — a view from the French as to how their minds also are working. Then in due course, I hope quite quickly, perhaps at another meeting or perhaps otherwise they will tell us what their reaction is and how they feel about it.'

For the benefit of the cameras I pulled out the Sud Aviation tie I was wearing, and concluded: 'Well, Mr Jenkins, did the French give you one of their very attractive Concorde ties while you were there?'

'No, they didn't. Perhaps that will come on the next visit.'

There were no more visits, however. President de Gaulle issued instructions that even the routine meetings between the British and French civil servants and technicians were to be suspended until the British came to their senses. The stalemate lasted for three months, with work at Toulouse in France and Filton in England gradually running down, I reported in a Christmas broadcast, 'in an atmosphere of anxiety pending official decisions on whether it's to be cancelled or continued'. I did my best to report the contest objectively, and to give the Government's point of view — but it seemed to me that America's determination to get rid of Concorde while pressing on with their own SST was clear evidence of the importance of retaining our stake in this long-term technological project.

The usual formula for shifting some of the responsibility for a deadlock was invoked: An eight-man committee headed by Lord Plowden was announced by Roy Jenkins to inquire whether Britain's aviation industry was bigger and more expensive than the country could afford, and there was a fruitless exchange of notes between the Foreign Office and the French. It was Julian Amery's no-break-clause Treaty, plus the energetic activities of the British and French trade unions who joined forces to insist on the project being continued, that finally saved Concorde. It was not, however, until the following February that the Wilson Government capitulated: Concorde could go ahead, but other projects — TSR2, the vertical take-off HS 1154 fighter and the HS 681 short take-off transport, would be cancelled.

And so it was not President Johnson, but President de Gaulle — whose long and supercilious nose, the cartoonists found, fitted the aircraft perfectly — who finally won the 1964 Battle for Concorde.

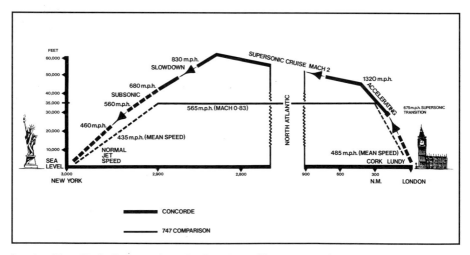

London-New York: Supersonic and subsonic profiles compared.

CHAPTER TWO

Concorde and the Big Bang

Grudgingly the French politicians forgave the British politicians for their abortive attempt to cancel Concorde, and some weeks later the Anglo-French engineers could stop pretending that they were no longer co-operating. The British and French Aviation Ministers (Roy Jonkins and M Jacquet) recovered their good humour over alternating lunches in Paris and London, and in February 1965 Najib Halaby, Head of the US Federal Aviation Administration (whose daughter, inheriting his good looks was to marry King Hussein and become Queen of Jordan), joined them. The far-sighted French also used the occasion to talk about the need for a 200-seat European airbus to complement Concorde and provide cheap travel for the masses, but this, as no doubt the French intended, was hardly noticed by the British. By then the US aircraft companies were spending about $2 million per month on their supersonic designs and pressing their Government for a go-ahead on construction. Officially Halaby came to discuss operational techniques and safety procedures, but he was probably more interested in spying out how Concorde was progressing technically as well as politically, since he admitted in a subsequent interview with me that Europe was two years ahead of the United States in supersonic technology.

Within days of this I was at Farnborough, describing an enormous facility nearing completion there, and which would ensure that the revolutionary Concorde would fly safely for — at the time of writing — at least 17 years after starting its passenger service.

Until the breakdown in Anglo-French relations the vast, cathedral-like structure had been known as the 'Concorde Facility'; when the aircraft's future looked doubtful, the complex was quietly redesignated Farnborough's new 'Structures Department', and the 'cathedral' itself became the Test Frame Laboratory. The RAE's monthly magazine carried a long enthusiastic article about it during the 'freeze' period with only one passing reference to Concorde right at the end. A year or two later Wernher von Braun, visiting Farnborough, confirmed its versatility by telling me enviously that it would be ideal for pre-flight testing of the Space Shuttle.

'This team in Farnborough has developed an absolutely unique capability which I think would benefit the Shuttle project tremendously,' he said. 'It could conceivably be a very important dowry that the British Government could bring into the Shuttle marriage, because this capability is not matched by anything that I know of in the USA . . . When you bite off an ambitious project like the Concorde, it benefits you not only in the immediate sense that you have a possibility and a chance of selling a good aeroplane, but also it gives you a leg-up on the next go-around.'

In due course the first Concorde airframe was towed in through the facility's 110ft wide, power-operated doors, to spend some five years being tested to destruction. Anchored to a floor able to withstand an upward pull of 500 tons, it was to be attached to cables and hawsers which would buffet and pull at it from 200 different points; infra-red heaters, using enough electricity for a town of 20,000 people, would 'barbecue' the airframe to match the 3-4hr periods of frictional heating which operational aircraft would endure during supersonic flight. Simulations of transatlantic flights were recycled endlessly, so that the test Concorde would always be at least five years ahead of those in passenger service. Many years earlier a similar large structure called 'Hercules' had been planned for testing airframes at Farnborough, and then cancelled as an economy measure.

The decision to build this facility was a direct result of the Comet disasters, and five years after construction began it seemed to have been given permanence and respectability with a formal opening by the Queen.

On my first visit however I was depressed by the accompanying rape of the countryside which I had so much enjoyed during my cycling days. 'The new building may be a Hampshire landmark — but try to drive there and it's as difficult to find as a needle in a haystack,' I said in an 'Eye-Witness' piece. 'It's right in the heart of this extraordinary, slummy area of Hampshire that's been created by the Services and Government establishments. You have to thread your way through tortuous lanes fringed by gorse, wet ditches and barbed wire. Large red notices threaten you with guard dogs on patrol — though I've never actually seen one. You come across Royal Engineers practising bridge-building, and armoured cars and rifle ranges.

'Jet planes on test, decorated with all sorts of funny bumps and lumps, scream low over your head as they skim the security fences protecting the vast Farnborough empire. But if you're lucky enough to come across the Government's National Gas Turbine Establishment at Pyestock, you're not far from Ball Hill and the new laboratory.'

Farnborough's scientists were well aware even then of the need to ensure that if Britain ever gave up making aircraft, their facilities would need to have other uses. 'Instead of aircraft, experimental buildings could be tested here,' my guide assured me.'All sorts of things could be tried out: for instance, whole sections of a possible English Channel bridge!'

None of these predictions came true. Successive Governments rejected any suggestion of getting involved in costly projects like the Space Shuttle, proposals for a Channel bridge came to nothing, and as this book appears, the apparently indestructible Structures Department is being demolished to make way for a new headquarters building for the Defence Research Agency.

The Structures Facility specially built at RAE Farnborough for a five year test-to-destruction of a full-size Concorde. It has ensured its safe performance ever since. Demolition of the facility started in 1993 to make way for a Headquarters Building for the Materials Dept of the Defence Research Agency. *RAE News*

Above: **Dr Wernher von Braun, rocket pioneer (right) wishing he could use the Structures Facility for Space Shuttle tests.** *RAE News*

Left: **A full-size Concorde being prepared for a five year test-to-destruction in the specially built Structures Facility at RAE Farnborough. The safety net in the centre was to prevent even a nut falling on the airframe.** *RAE News*

April 1965: First metal was cut for Concorde prototypes. Here tape-controlled machining is underway Filton for a window panel section. *BAC*

'Exercise Westminster', the first public demonstration of what Concorde's sonic bangs *might* sound like, was allegedly laid on by the Ministry of Aviation because so many members of Parliament had asked for it. But like most Ministry activities, its real motives were suspect — and in the case of Concorde motivated by a Civil Service desire to distance itself from the whole project, and establish a 'We-did-tell-you' alibi against final cancellation.

That view is supported by the fact that of 1,200 peers and MPs invited to attend the demonstration, only four peers and 15 MPs actually turned up.

We gathered on a cold, windy day at the RAF Upwood Station in Huntingdonshire — 250 of us. Media people like me had our tape recorders for radio, and camera crews for TV, and, having its traditional little joke, Whitehall issued the Press with yellow badges.

Other guests, including fascinated aviation experts from Italy, France and America, as well as Britain's pilots' organisations, building experts, local government representatives, and, most worried of all, insurance representatives were given white badges. Intrepid Ministry men wore blue (true-blue?) badges.

Handel Davies, the Ministry of Aviation scientist responsible for aircraft research and development — a friendly, open man — assured me that the object was to make the worst sort of bangs — creating an 'overpressure' on the eardrums of about 2lb per square foot — likely to be experienced by people living under the flight paths of supersonic aircraft.

Everyone was issued with a little booklet explaining the 'scientific background' and the fact that the double bang usually heard was caused by the shock waves from the bow and stern of the aircraft. It also revealed that the bang was heard at all points on the ground below and on either side of the aircraft for a distance of up to 20 miles, the intensity depending upon the altitude and weight of the aircraft, and to a lesser extent upon its shape and speed, wind and temperature conditions, ground terrain, location of buildings, etc. A centre page spread headed 'Record of Events' invited us to keep 'a personal record of events as they occur'.

Half the bangs, listed A to L, were to be heard outdoors in the morning, followed by a restorative buffet lunch in the Officers' Mess and another A to L sequence to be heard indoors in the afternoon.

There were eight genuine supersonic bangs made by Lightning fighters flying at nearly 1,000mph five miles above us, costing the taxpayer £500 each; interspersed were eight 'simulated' bangs made by firing half-pound charges of explosive costing only £1.50 each. I polled the peers and MPs on their reactions, which varied from scepticism to reassurance. The sceptics thought the bangs would be a good deal worse when made by Concorde itself. Concorde's developers were hoping the bangs would be so reassuring that they could go ahead with enlarging the aircraft — which of course would increase the bang. The British wanted to add another 20 seats to the 118 planned, to improve its profitability. The French thought an additional 8-10 seats was all that would be possible.

My problems when it came to covering supersonic bangs proved insuperable. Recording engineers on the spot, and those in the studio when it came to transmission, turned down their 'pots' just before the bangs, in the first case to avoid 'overloading' the magnetic tape, which resulted in little more than a click when it was played back. The inside engineers turned their volumes down at the critical moment because they had been trained for years not to frighten the public with sudden bangs — which might also damage their receivers.

So, by the time they reached listeners and viewers our expensively recorded supersonic bangs were either completely inaudible or no more than a distant 'pop'. Between them, then and ever after, they made it impossible for me to tell an honest story!

My scripts show that as the demonstration progressed I interviewed Aviation Minister Roy Jenkins; as usual he was guarded and non-committal, but I do not have a transcription of what he actually said. For comparison, a Ministry of Aviation Comet made a low flypast, which led me to comment in my TV report: 'As a personal opinion, I'd sooner have occasional supersonic bangs than noise like this that can drown speech — and the TV — for half a minute at a time.'

A few weeks later, on a visit to Toulouse to see the steady growth of Concorde 001, the first prototype, I also had my first meeting with the man selected to make the first flight in it. He was Andre Turcat, bald, tall and ramrod straight in the French equivalent of a Savile Row suit. He was the ultimate Frenchman with sufficient qualities of confidence, style and elegance to intimidate the most self-satisfied Briton.

'How does one prepare to be the pilot of the world's first supersonic aircraft?' I asked him.

'It's not only a job for just a pilot, or even a test pilot, but for an engineer too. And in my case I am also director of the flight test department of Sud Aviation. So I am responsible for every flight test.'

'The French Concorde will fly about six months before Britain's first Concorde. How has that happened?'

'The decision was made by the Committee of Directors. I think that this is due mainly to the fact that the technical direction for the project is French.'

'And when you make the maiden flight will Godfrey Auty, Britain's test pilot on the Concorde, be with you?'

'No, I don't think so. It's obvious that not only Godfrey Auty but other crew members of the British Aircraft Corporation will have the opportunity to fly in the first prototype before flying the No.2, but generally speaking, apart from information or training, I don't think it would be right to have mixed crews. Our first aim is efficiency, so I think that even if in a later stage the BAC crew has to fly the No.1, it would still be more useful to have homogeneous crews.'

'Well, you're 43 now and you'll be 47 when the first flight is made. Is that rather old do you think for the first supersonic pilot?'

Turcat laughed. 'How could I answer that it's rather old? There is no ideal age. Every man has his own best age...I hope to be young enough.'

I asked him about likely public reaction to supersonic flight. For instance would it be hard to persuade women to start flying in these very fast aircraft?

'I don't think so. People are always interested in speed, and this will arouse more enthusiasm than fear, even for women.'

'So you think everybody will soon enjoy supersonic flight?'

'Maybe not everybody at the beginning, but I am sure that this will be the case after a few months.'

Soon after that interview Godfrey Auty, then Chief Test Pilot of BAC's Filton Division, where Concorde 002 was being assembled, who had told me himself

Forward fuselage for 001 under construction at Filton — later sent to Toulouse for final assembly. *BAC*

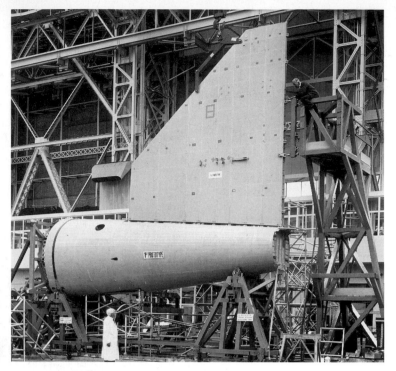

Left: **001's fin, made at BAC Weybridge, is mated at Filton with the rear fuselage, which was made at BAC Preston, before despatch to Toulouse for final assembly.** *BAC*

Below: **Test rig at Filton, built by a shipbuilder, capable of moving Concorde wings into any flight position and used to investigate effects of fuel transfers between tanks.** *BAC*

that he would be making the maiden flight, was replaced by Brian Trubshaw. How that happened is somewhat obscure, but Trubshaw had been test pilot with Vickers under Sir George Edwards at Weybridge since 1950. Sir George was always intensely loyal to his own staff, and probably gave Trubshaw preference for that reason.

Concorde construction had progressed so far by the end of 1965 that confidence began to grow among the world's airlines that this aircraft really would fly — whereas in the US there were still no decisions about what sort of supersonic plane they would tackle.

As a result Japan Air Lines, which had given provisional orders for a US supersonic plane but held back on Concorde, decided to join the Anglo-French queue. The airline's president signed up for three 'options', bringing the total to over 50, explaining that now Concorde's range was to be over 4,000 miles with 134 passengers, they could use it on major routes like Tokyo to Honolulu.

BAC and Sud Aviation had to endure regular high-level visits of inspection by their potential customers, and in February 1966, Charles Tillinghast, head of TWA, after visiting the factories, was warning that Concorde was in danger of pricing itself out of the market. He admitted that America's projected SST was three years behind and would cost twice as much — over £10 millions. But he said that its 200-passenger seats compared with Concorde's possible 136, and its 2,000mph compared with Concorde's 1,500, would enable the American aircraft to do twice as much work. He surprised his Anglo-French hosts even more by asserting that, despite its larger size, the US aircraft would make a slightly smaller sonic bang than Concorde. It was an instructive example of the ability of US salesmen to convince their customers about the performance of an aircraft which had not yet been selected from among three contenders.

Little was made of the US Government's dilemma about how to fund the development of their SST. For once a future civil airliner could not be developed on the back of a military plane paid for out of the defence budget; and the planemakers were making it very clear that there was no hope that they could raise the money as they had done for the Boeing 707 and DC10, and were doing for the 747 Jumbo Jet. Civil servants in the State Department consulted with those in the Federal Aviation Adminmistration and came up with the answer: the airlines must pay! Twelve US airlines which had ordered a total of 57 US SSTs were reluctantly persuaded to pay $1 million (then equivalent to £300,000) for each aircraft ordered — not as part of the purchase price, but as a contribution to the £500 million needed to build the two prototypes. This meant that Pan American, which had ordered 15, had to pay the lion's share. As a way of discouraging any more orders, and provoking cancellation of some already placed, the idea worked brilliantly.

There was then, as I reported in March from Seattle, a fierce argument between the FAA and the State Department as to whether it would be ethical to ask the foreign airline customers to back their orders in the same way — and, if they refused, to tell them that they had lost the places in the production 'queue' that they had already booked for the US SST. It would have meant that BOAC and Air France would each have to pay £2 million to help finance America's SST, when they had paid nothing for their options on the European product.

Boeings had flown the British air correspondents to Seattle to show us a £3 million mockup of their proposed aircraft, and they certainly succeeded in taking

Meanwhile Sud Aviation fuselage components arrive at Filton to complete assembly of 002. *BAC*

our breath away. BBC television was then changing from black and white to colour, so in addition to my radio pieces I had to do two TV versions — one in monochrome and one in colour. I made it hard for myself by persuading the camera crew to set up in the open emergency escape hatch on to the 180ft wing, and then talking to camera as I walked towards it from the wingtip:

'Experts say this breath-taking rival to Concorde will create a quarter of a million new jobs for American aviation workers in the next 10 years. That should make it available for passenger service in mid-1974 — less than three years behind Concorde. It's a hundred yards long — and when cruising at 1,800mph the intense heat will make it stretch another eight inches . . . The double droop-snoot nose, to make sure the pilots can see for take off, landing and taxying, and the swinging wings, make Boeing's supersonic far more complex than Concorde. The wing pivots are made of titanium bearings and stainless steel; and a great ball screw, needing three engines to drive it, will sweep the wings back for supersonic flight, forwards for landing and take-off. And for the pilot, 16ft up and far ahead of his wheels, there'll be television to help. Cameras mounted under the tail will give *this* view, so that he can watch the ground and wheels for touch-down and taxying . . . Even before the go-ahead, 1,500 designers and technicians are working flat out, preparing for production. They've even planned bigger seats, because passengers in the 1970s will be one inch taller and 10 pounds heavier.'

That reference to bigger seats must evoke hollow laughter from passengers unable to move their knees in the charter planes of the 1990s. At the time I found it difficult to believe that the great Boeing firm, with so much practical achievement behind it, really expected us to believe in this unlikely monster. And by then the talk was that each of these aircraft would cost £15 millions — a 50% increase on the price Tillinghast had quoted a few months back.

Sir Giles Guthrie, the merchant-banker baronet who had been appointed as Chairman of BOAC with a brief to make it pay for itself, had cancelled most of the VC10 orders, and shown little enthusiasm for Concorde, unexpectedly waxed lyrical about it during a visit to Australia. He surprised the accompanying air correspondents by referring to 'this spectacular aeroplane...an airline planner's dream' and said it would be put straight on a round-the-world-service to Australia, taking 33hr including stops. But next day he disclosed that he was worried about its operating costs, and complained that the Department of Economic Affairs had failed to comply with his requests to see a report on the subject compiled with information from the Ministry of Technology and the Anglo-French planemakers.

Had more notice been taken of these reports, the update on Concorde given to the public at the Farnborough Air Show in September that year might have come as less of a shock. Fred Mulley had a chat over lunch in the President's tent with his opposite number from France, then M. Pisani, Minister of Equipment, and they announced afterwards that estimated costs had jumped from £340 millions to £500 millions. Additional development costs had added £80 millions, and another £50 millions had been included as contingency — or, as I described it, 'just-in-case' money. But with options from airlines then totalling 60, we were reassured that the 'break even point' of 100 might be reached before the end of the year.

Evidence that all these estimates were based upon some real work was provided just before the end of Farnborough when a Vulcan V-bomber made two low passes to show the public that it had been fitted with an 8-ton pod beneath the bomb-bay labelled 'Bristol Siddeley Olympus'. This was the start of a flight test programme to see how Concorde's engine would behave when flown subsonically; because the TSR2 had been cancelled, supersonic testing would not be possible until the first Concorde prototype started flying in 1968.

A Lockheed news conference held in London shortly afterwards received much less coverage than the jump in Concorde development costs. Lockheed had decided that Concorde would be a success.

This company also considered they were more likely to get the expected US Government contract to develop the rival supersonic airliner — and certainly their double-delta proposal looked a lot more practical than Boeing's double-droop-snoot, swing-wing project, which appeared to my non-technical eye to be a monstrosity which would never fly. What was of most interest to Britain and France, however, was Lockheed's independent estimate that 316 Concordes would be sold by 1985, and that by that time 907 of their bigger, 250-passenger supersonic transports would have been sold. This gave some authority to BAC's argument that if only the Government would provide even more money for them to tool up to produce five instead of two Concordes per month, they would be able to sell at least 500.

Incidentally, Carl Kotchian, the Lockheed executive who had come to Britain seeking BOAC orders for his SST had a new definition of its anticipated sonic boom for those who would be living under it: it would merely sound like somebody closing a car door.

No doubt it was this prospect of success that led the Labour government to appoint their own Director-General-Concorde, his brief being to keep a firm hand on costs, and to co-ordinate the Government side of research and development at their own aircraft and jet engine establishments. He was James Hamilton, a senior civil servant with a scientific background — a happy man who quickly established good relations with the air correspondents as well as the Anglo-French aviation industry, and who was one of the very few who got a knighthood out of the project!

Jim Hamilton quickly made his mark. He had to deal with two ministers and briefly two ministries, because the doomed John Stonehouse, the last and shortest-lived Minister of Aviation, was at the time having his Ministry and its staff of over 30,000 taken over and merged into that of Anthony Wedgwood Benn's Ministry of Technology, which was only one quarter of the size. It also led to Stonehouse being downgraded to Minister of State under Wedgwood Benn (the former hereditary Viscount Stansgate, who insisted on becoming 'Tony Benn'). Jim Hamilton, ignoring these complications, and no doubt mainly at the instigation of Benn, decided it was time to prepare the public ('educate them, if you like' I said on TV News), by subjecting them to unannounced sonic booms. Both France and America had already carried out such experiments: in Oklahoma there had been 1,200 sonic booms which had brought 12,000 complaints and claims for compensation — some genuine for broken windows in tall buildings, some of them claims for damage allegedly caused by booms which never happened — hence the decision not to announce Britain's booms in advance.

After some of us had discovered the plan, Stonehouse confirmed it in the House and said there would be about one boom a day in a different area each

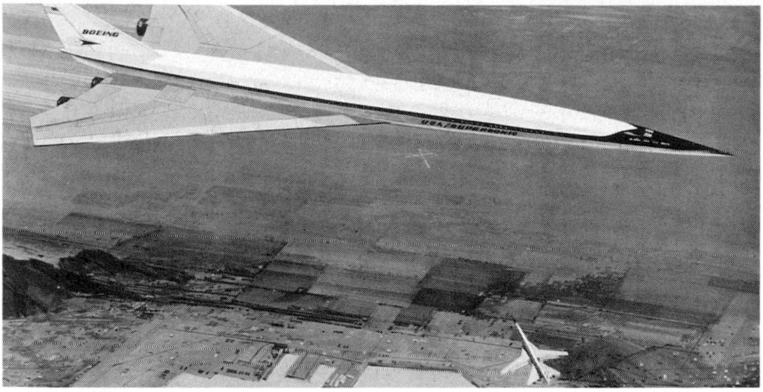

Left: **Artist's impression of proposed Boeing 2707 swing-wing, double droop-snoot SST. It is shown cruising, with wings swept, and below, with wings extended for landing.**
J. M. Ramsden

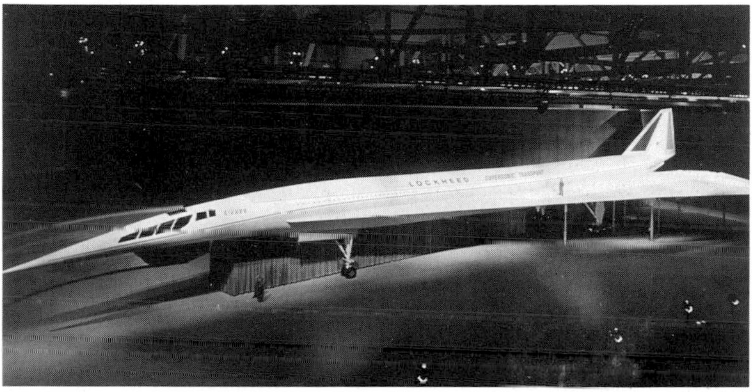

Left: **Rival Lockheed SST proposal was similar in appearance to Concorde, but twice as big.**
J. M. Ramsden

Below: ***Sunday Observer* for 5 June 1966 headed 'The Menace of the Boom' with inset picture of *Bo Lundberg*.**

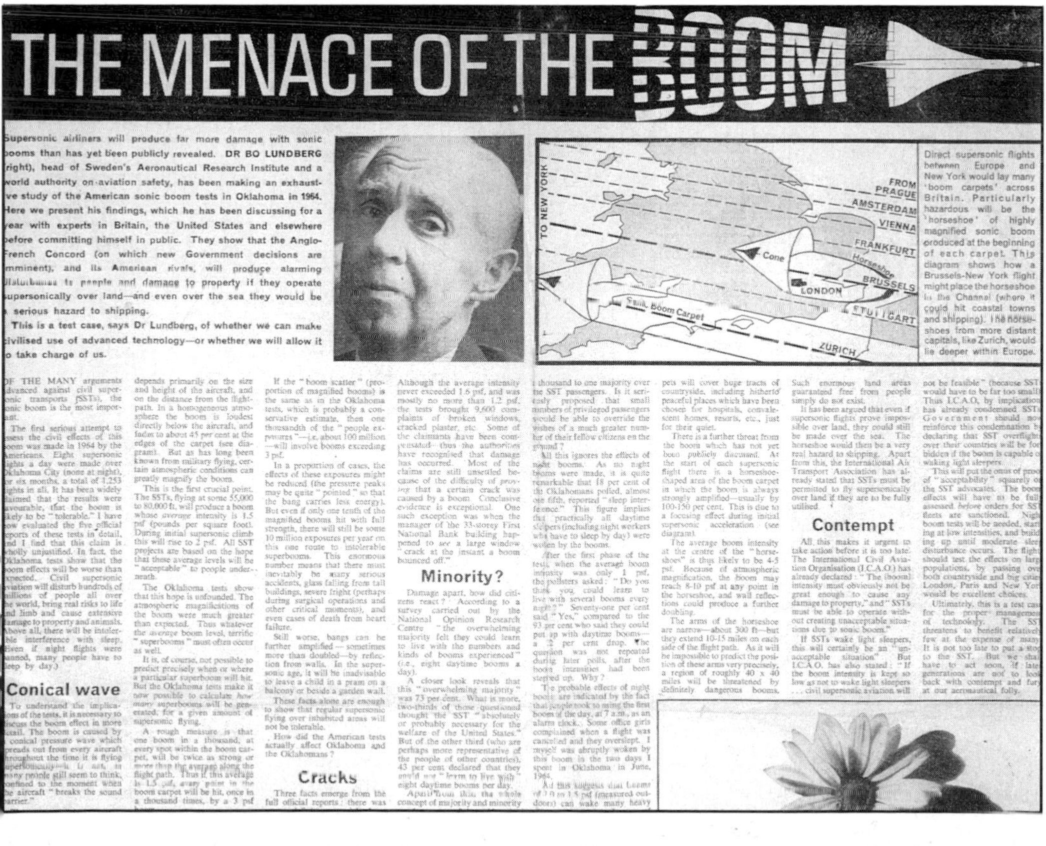

THE MENACE OF THE BOOM

Supersonic airliners will produce far more damage with sonic booms than has yet been publicly revealed. DR BO LUNDBERG (right), head of Sweden's Aeronautical Research Institute and a world authority on aviation safety, has been making an exhaustive study of the American sonic boom tests in Oklahoma in 1964. Here we present his findings, which he has been discussing for a year with experts in Britain, the United States and elsewhere before committing himself in public. They show that the Anglo-French Concord (on which new Government decisions are imminent), and its American rivals, will produce alarming disturbance to people and damage to property if they operate supersonically over land—and even over the sea they would be a serious hazard to shipping.

This is a test case, says Dr Lundberg, of whether we can make civilised use of advanced technology—or whether we will allow it to take charge of us.

Direct supersonic flights between Europe and New York would lay many 'boom carpets' across Britain. Particularly hazardous will be the 'horseshoe' of highly magnified sonic boom produced at the beginning of each carpet. This diagram shows how a Brussels-New York flight might place the horseshoe in the Channel (where it could hit coastal towns and shipping). The horseshoes from more distant capitals, like Zurich, would lie deeper within Europe.

OF THE MANY arguments advanced against civil supersonic transports (SSTs), the sonic boom is the most important.

The first serious attempt to assess the civil effects of this boom was made in 1964 by the Americans. Eight supersonic flights a day were made over Oklahoma City (none at night), for six months, a total of 1,253 flights in all. It has been widely claimed that the results were favourable, that the boom is likely to be "tolerable." I have now evaluated the five official reports of these tests in detail, and I find that this claim is wholly unjustified. In fact, the Oklahoma tests show that the boom effects will be worse than expected. Civil supersonic aviation will disturb hundreds of millions of people all over the world, bring real risks to life and limb and cause extensive damage to property and animals. Above all, there will be intolerable interference with sleep. (Even if night flights were banned, many people have to sleep by day.)

Conical wave

To understand the implications of the tests, it is necessary to discuss the boom effect in more detail. The boom is caused by a conical pressure wave which spreads out from every aircraft throughout the time it is flying supersonically—it is not, as many people still seem to think, confined to the moment when the aircraft "breaks the sound barrier."

... depends primarily on the size and height of the aircraft, and on the distance from the flight-path. In a homogeneous atmosphere the boom is loudest directly below the aircraft, and fades to about 45 per cent at the edges of the carpet (see diagram). But as has long been known from military flying, certain atmospheric conditions can greatly magnify the boom.

This is the first crucial point. The SSTs, flying at some 55,000 to 80,000 ft, will produce a boom whose *average* intensity is 1.5 psf (pounds per square foot). During initial supersonic climb this will rise to 2 psf. All SST projects are based on the hope that these average levels will be "acceptable" to people underneath.

The Oklahoma tests show that this hope is unfounded. The atmospheric magnifications of the boom were much greater than expected. Thus whatever the *average* boom level, terrific "superbooms" must often occur as well.

It is, of course, not possible to predict precisely when or where a particular superboom will hit. But the Oklahoma tests make it now possible to calculate *how many* superbooms will be generated, for a given amount of supersonic flying.

A rough measure is that one boom in a thousand, at every spot within the boom carpet, will be twice as strong or more than the average along the flight path. Thus if this average is 1.5 psf, every point in the boom carpet will be hit, once in a thousand times, by a 3 psf boom.

If the "boom scatter" (proportion of magnified booms) is the same as in the Oklahoma tests, which is probably a conservative estimate, then one thousandth of the "people exposures"—i.e. about 100 million—will involve booms exceeding 3 psf.

In a proportion of cases, the effects of these exposures might be reduced (the pressure peaks may be quite "pointed" so that the bang carries less energy). But even if only one tenth of the magnified booms hit with full strength, there will still be some 10 million exposures per year on this one route to intolerable superbooms. This enormous number means that there must inevitably be many serious accidents, glass falling from tall buildings, severe fright (perhaps during surgical operations and other critical moments), and even cases of death from heart failure.

Still worse, bangs can be further amplified—sometimes more than doubled—by reflection from walls. In the supersonic age, it will be inadvisable to leave a child in a pram on a balcony or beside a garden wall.

These facts alone are enough to show that regular supersonic flying over inhabited areas will not be tolerable.

How did the American tests actually affect Oklahoma and the Oklahomans?

Cracks

Three facts emerge from the full official reports: there was ...

Although the average intensity never exceeded 1.6 psf, and was mostly no more than 1.2 psf, the tests brought 9,600 complaints of broken windows, cracked plaster, etc. Some of the claimants have been compensated—thus the authorities have recognised that damage has occurred. Most of the claims are still unsettled because of the difficulty of *proving* that a certain crack was caused by a boom. Conclusive evidence is exceptional. One such exception was when the manager of the 33-storey First National Bank building happened to *see* a large window "crack at the instant a boom bounced off."

Minority?

Damage apart, how did citizens react? According to a survey carried out by the National Opinion Research Centre "the overwhelming majority felt they could learn to live with the numbers and kinds of booms experienced" (i.e., eight daytime booms a day).

A closer look reveals that this "overwhelming majority" was 73 per cent. What is more, two-thirds of those questioned thought the SST "absolutely or probably necessary for the welfare of the United States." But of the other third (who are perhaps more representative of the people of other countries), 43 per cent declared that they would not "learn to live with" eight daytime booms per day.

Apart from this, the whole concept of majority and minority ... a thousand to one majority over the SST passengers. Is it seriously proposed that small numbers of privileged passengers should be able to override the wishes of a much greater number of their fellow citizens on the ground?

All this ignores the effects of night booms. As no night booms were made, it is quite remarkable that 18 per cent of the Oklahomans polled, almost one fifth, reported "sleep interference." This figure implies that practically all daytime sleepers (including night workers who have to sleep by day) were woken by the booms.

After the first phase of the tests, when the average boom intensity was only 1 psf, the pollsters asked: "Do you think you could learn to live with several booms every night?" Seventy-one per cent said "Yes," compared to the 93 per cent who said they could put up with daytime booms—a 22 per cent drop. The question was not repeated during later polls, after the boom intensities had been stepped up. Why?

The probable effects of night booms are indicated by the fact that people took to using the first boom of the day, at 7 a.m., as an alarm clock. Some office girls complained when a flight was cancelled and they overslept. I myself was abruptly woken by this boom in the two days I spent in Oklahoma in June, 1964.

All this suggests that booms of 1.0 to 1.5 psf (measured outdoors) can wake many heavy ...

... pets will cover huge tracts of countryside, including hitherto peaceful places which have been chosen for hospitals, convalescent homes, resorts, etc., just for their quiet.

There is a further threat from the boom which has not yet been publicly discussed. At the start of each supersonic flight there is a horseshoe-shaped area of the boom carpet in which the boom is always strongly amplified—usually by 100-150 per cent. This is due to a focusing effect during initial supersonic acceleration (see diagram).

The average boom intensity at the centre of the "horseshoes" is thus likely to be 4-5 psf. Because of atmospheric magnification, the boom may reach 8-10 psf at any point in the horseshoe, and wall reflections could produce a further doubling.

The arms of the horseshoe are narrow—about 300 ft—but they extend 10-15 miles on each side of the flight path. As it will be impossible to predict the position of these arms very precisely, a region of roughly 40 x 40 miles will be threatened by definitely dangerous booms. Such enormous land areas guaranteed free from people simply do not exist.

It has been argued that even if supersonic flights prove impossible over land, they could still be made over the sea. The horseshoe would then be a very real hazard to shipping. Apart from this, the International Air Transport Association has already stated that SSTs must be permitted to fly supersonically over land if they are to be fully utilised.

Contempt

All this makes it urgent to take action before it is too late. The International Civil Aviation Organisation (I.C.A.O.) has already declared: "The (boom) intensity must obviously not be great enough to cause any damage to property," and "SSTs must be able to operate without creating unacceptable situations due to sonic boom."

If SSTs wake light sleepers, this will certainly be an "unacceptable situation." But I.C.A.O. has also stated: "If the boom intensity is kept so low as not to wake light sleepers . . . civil supersonic aviation will not be feasible" (because SSTs would have to be far too small). Thus I.C.A.O., by implication, has already condemned SSTs. Government should now reinforce this condemnation by declaring that SST overflights over their countries will be forbidden if the boom is capable of waking light sleepers.

This will put the onus of proof of "acceptability" squarely on the SST advocates. The boom effects will have to be fully assessed *before* orders for SST fleets are sanctioned. Night boom tests will be needed, starting at low intensities, and building up until moderate sleep disturbance occurs. The flights should test the effects on large populations, by passing over both countryside and big cities. London, Paris and New York would be excellent choices.

Ultimately, this is a test case for the proper management of technology. The SST threatens to benefit relatively few at the expense of many. It is not too late to put a stop to the SST. But we shall have to act soon, if later generations are not to look back with contempt and fury at our aeronautical folly.

time, made by a Lightning fighter flying at an altitude of eight miles and at 1,000mph. How similar this would be to Concorde's boom no one would know until that aircraft flew (and when that time came Concorde's proved to be far heavier, and quite intolerable over populated areas). The first Lightning boom came three days later, and the Ministry of Technology refused to give an exact location because their technical experts said it would affect the reliability of any complaints. However, after a few minutes on the telephone I discovered that a Lightning fighter had taken off from Boscombe Down and made a supersonic bang over Blandford in Dorset, just 20 miles away. Many newspapers also identified the area, and the Ministry was not pleased. Things got very confused, and I enjoyed myself on the 'Today' programme:

'The Government told us that because we were paying for Concorde we were entitled to take part in some sonic boom tests — to judge for ourselves what it would be like to have supersonic airliners passing overhead faster than the speed of sound. But the experts' idea of letting us "join in" these tests is to impose them on us without warning, and then refuse even to tell us if it was a sonic boom that we heard. It was only under pressure that the Ministry of Technology admitted that if the public wanted to complain about a sonic boom — or even to tell someone they thought they'd heard one — it was their ministry they should tell. In fact, for a public exercise, the operation couldn't be more secret if it was covered by a D-notice... If the public aren't prepared to put up with it, supersonic airliners like Concorde and its American rival will only be allowed to fly supersonically over the sea. It's what the politicians call "public reaction" that will in the end decide. And presumably no official explanation has been given to the public in case it affects the way they react. But how about a bit of practice?'

My script ended: 'ACTUALITY: Two more sonic bangs' but as always the production assistants in the gallery hurriedly turned down their volume controls just before the recording went out, so as not to alarm the elderly and sensitive, and the whole effect of the broadcast was destroyed !

There were only eleven sonic booms in this series of tests, most of them over Bristol, because Tony Benn felt it only right that the people living in the area where Concorde was being built and providing thousands of jobs should know about the disadvantages of the project. We were told that about 100 claims followed for damage for broken windows, fallen and cracked ceilings, losses due to shocked hens refusing to lay eggs, the milk curdling in cows' udders, etc.

Ultimately compensation payments of £4,000 were made. From the politicians' point of view the campaign was brought to a dramatic climax by subjecting the Greater London area to the last four. The first came from a Lightning flying northwards across London. Margaret, washing up in our house at Sydenham, rang me to say it was 'quite frightening', and was duly quoted in my first report. Two days later came another boom, caused by the same pilot flying east-to-west along the course of the Thames. There was general disappointment that MPs in the House were making so much of their own noise that they did not hear it, but everyone else appeared to do so. Was this boom less severe because the aircraft was higher, as most of us suspected, or because of different weather conditions? Another unanswered question. Around this time the pioneering sailor Sir Francis Chichester, knighted in recognition of his single-handed ocean voyages, was welcomed at

36

Tower Bridge with a salute of guns, which many people mistook for sonic booms and complained about to the Ministry — thus, said their spokesmen smugly, justifying their policy of not announcing them.

The final boom, on 21 July 1967, was turned into a political 'event'. It was announced the day before, so that the sophisticated London public at least would have a chance to make a considered judgement as to whether they could learn to live with such booms.

Tony Benn apparently preferred the neutrality of his luxurious office; but John Stonehouse, Jim Hamilton, and Wing Commander Merriman, officer commanding the Lightnings charged with creating the booms, assembled on the rooftop of the Ministry of Technology in Whitehall to hear the climactic bang. They made sure of course that we of the media were also there to record them hearing it. It came two minutes early.

At that height, I reported, it sounded like a double pistol shot, whereas people at street level mostly heard a single, reverberating bang. I interviewed all three 'VIPs', and Stonehouse said that complaints about broken windows, etc, were being investigated 'but not necessarily accepted'.

While all this was going on, anti-Concorde and anti-supersonic movements were growing under the stimulus of several prophets of doom.

One was Professor Bo Lundberg, former test pilot and by then Director of Sweden's Aeronautical Research Institute. Swift destruction by hailstones and slow destruction by radiation — especially in the case of pregnant women — were two dangers he posed for those bold enough to travel supersonically. Richard Wiggs, a Hertfordshire schoolmaster, effectively harnessed the protest movement in Britain, which attracted progressive movements — although the Communists became somewhat confused because the Soviet Union was also working on a supersonic aircraft.

The protest movements were much stimulated by a report around that time that a French farmer, his wife and a neighbour had died in their farmhouse near Rennes, Brittany, when the old house was allegedly shaken by a sonic boom, with the result that an ancient beam gave way and they were buried in eight tons of barley which had been stored in the loft above them. Little attention was devoted to the thought that the loft could well have been grossly overloaded and the beams neglected; but stories multiplied of towers and ancient churches having to be shored up, with the glories of their stained glass windows under constant threat. In England it was thought that transatlantic flights would take Concordes over or near the tip of Cornwall, and people who had never before heard of Truro Cathedral began campaigning against the prospect of its imminent collapse.

That summer in London was to have been enlivened with the presence in Battersea Park of a full-scale mockup of Concorde which had been the highlight of the Paris Air Show, attracting bigger queues to walk through it than Lenin's tomb in Red Square. No doubt Britain had paid half the £250,000 cost of building the mockup, and it was going to cost another £25,000 to bring it by barge down the Seine and up the Thames to Battersea. I had a mental picture of the TV pieces I would do, in monochrome and colour, chronicling the journey by the slowest means of transport of this full-size mockup of the world's fastest aircraft. It would clearly be a splendid public relations exercise, allowing the British public to enjoy their share in the project. There was no doubt that, as in France,

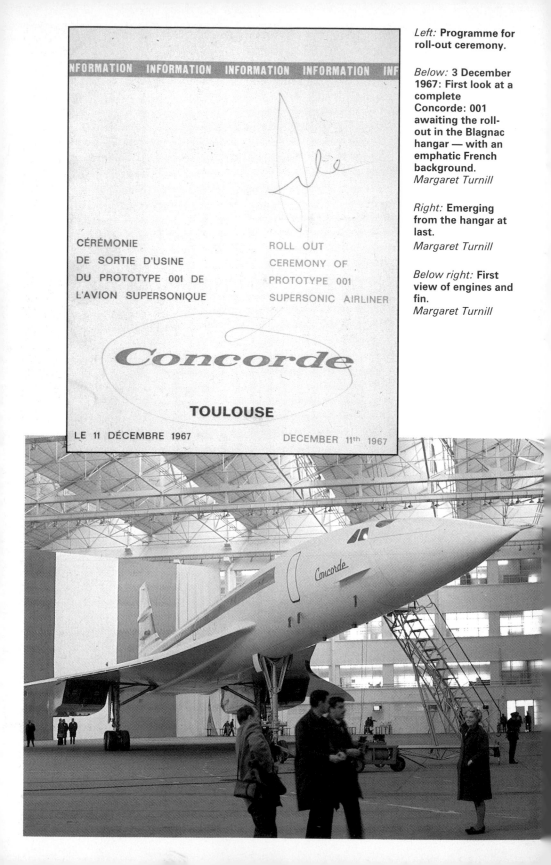

INFORMATION INFORMATION INFORMATION INFORMATION INF

CÉRÉMONIE
DE SORTIE D'USINE
DU PROTOTYPE 001 DE
L'AVION SUPERSONIQUE

ROLL OUT
CEREMONY OF
PROTOTYPE 001
SUPERSONIC AIRLINER

Concorde

TOULOUSE

LE 11 DÉCEMBRE 1967   DECEMBER 11th 1967

Left: **Programme for roll-out ceremony.**

Below: **3 December 1967: First look at a complete Concorde: 001 awaiting the roll-out in the Blagnac hangar — with an emphatic French background.**
Margaret Turnill

Right: **Emerging from the hangar at last.**
Margaret Turnill

Below right: **First view of engines and fin.**
Margaret Turnill

With droop snoot removed, 001 is towed across Blagnac airfield after the roll-out.
Sud Aviation

thousands would gladly pay two shillings each (about 50p in the 1990s) to walk through it.

When it had not arrived two months after the Paris Air Show I asked why. There had been 'unexpected difficulties', I was told by BAC and the Ministry of Technology. I had to exercise the usual newsman's persistence before I learned that the French were saying it was not possible to send it after all. Unfortunately (they said) they had had to make the model in such a hurry for the Paris Air Show that it had not been possible to make it in sections to enable it to be dismantled for transport on the barge! The unofficial British view, which I shared despite hot French denials, was that French policy was to foster the general belief on the Continent that Concorde was really a French rather than Anglo-French project, and transferring the model so publicly might dispel this belief. It disappeared into a Le Bourget hangar until the fuss died down, was bought the following year for half a million francs (£38,000) by the French Airports Authority, and has continued to be a major visitor attraction at Le Bourget, still generating queues during the biennial Air Show, ever since!

In May, with 70 other journalists from 15 countries, I saw Concorde 001 in the final assembly stage at Toulouse, and was given a warning by Bernard Dufour, the French production chief, which I reported, but which I should have relied upon the following February.

There were big technical problems still to be surmounted, he said, and there was no spare time for overcoming unexpected problems if it were to be ready for the scheduled first flight on 28 February 1968.

In November 300 pilots gathered in London to seek assurances, among other things that they would not be held personally responsible for any sonic boom damage. The Foreign Office had issued visas for a group of Soviet pilots training to fly the Tu-144, but as so often happened in those days they did not turn up. John Stonehouse did turn up however, to say that he had recently walked on the wing of the Soviet prototype, and that Soviet designers had told him that the Tu-144 would also fly early the next year. However, added Stone-house, Britain had increased its lead over the US to four years, and should have 150 Concordes in airline service before they got started.

Everyone on the production side, but most of all BAC's public relations manager, Charles Gardner (whose dislike of me, his successor at the BBC, had become incandescent and was to a lesser extent returned), was desperate to maintain this spirit of optimism two weeks before Christmas, when we were all summoned to Blagnac, near Toulouse, for the great roll out ceremony. Accompanied by disapproval from BBC programme chiefs, because it meant I was out of touch for two days before and after the event, my wife Margaret and I drove there in our new Vauxhall Victor, one of the nicest cars we ever had; its combined heating and ventilation system never has been surpassed in any car we have had since, and we got the full benefit on the long return journey because the temperature was five degrees Fahrenheit below freezing, and the roads were treacherous with compacted snow.

We checked into Le Bristol, a small hotel on the outskirts of Toulouse next door to Le Concorde, two days before the ceremony in order to do some 'scene-setters' beloved by all good TV deskmen.

Their great value is that if (usually 'when') the film or video of the actual happening fails to reach the studio in time, they can fall back on the 'scene setter'. As for Le Bristol, it had many advantages: not only was its charge for a double room well within my BBC daily allowance; its other guests included many senior British engineers and technicians seconded to Sud Aviation from companies like Boulton Paul and Bristol Siddeley.

They provided material for my first scene-setter within five minutes of my taking a stool at the bar. The food was superb too, and after enjoying that we decided to recover from the long drive with an early night in our huge, ornately-ceilinged bedroom on the ground floor. Soon after midnight we were awoken from a deep sleep by thunderous and menacing noises familiar from the London blitz, and apparently heralding the end of the world. When the crashing and shaking ceased and we cautiously poked our heads above the blankets, the room was full of dust, but otherwise seemed intact. Cautiously I opened the door. The corridor was a foot deep in rubble from what had been a magnificent 15ft high plaster ceiling and which after a couple of neglected centuries, had chosen this moment to fall without even the excuse of a sonic boom. To our surprise no one appeared, so we clambered over it and made our way along to the bar. It was packed, and the exuberant occupants were making so much noise of their own that if they had heard anything they paid it no attention. The noise died, however, as some of them, peering through the blue haze of smoke and garlic, drew attention to the odd couple in their nightclothes in the doorway. Margaret broke a silence deep enough to hear a pin drop with the dramatic words: 'Le plafond est tombé!'

With that we retreated, to be followed shortly after by an alcoholic surge of Concorde employees. We left them uttering cries of 'Mon Dieu' and — in the case of the staff, who had to start a major clearing operation at 1am — 'Quelle horreur!' and went back to our gritty bed.

My first story next day was that, in sharp contrast to roll-out ceremonies in Britain and America, the workers had been forbidden to attend. The French employees had been instructed to come in at 6am, do half a day's work, and be clear of the Sud works by 10am; the British fitters, electricians and inspectors were told to take the whole day off — but were so angry at not being allowed to attend the ceremony they were threatening to go back to Bristol. The media too was to suffer from such draconian orders, issued in the name of efficiency and security by Maurice Papon, who had replaced the popular Andre Puget as French head of the Concorde project. Maybe because he had been too friendly with his British opposite numbers like Sir George Edwards, Puget had been suddenly banished to the role of Ambassador to Sweden, and his job given to the former Prefect of the Paris Police. So greatly was Papon feared, that the world's media had been given a small room on the 4th floor of the Blagnac air-field office block — and forbidden to use the lift in case Papon himself might need it at some time. This was especially hard on the TV crews. In the case of the BBC, working in both monochrome and colour film, they had to carry all their heavy equipment up and down the stairs.

Fortunately we had already 'canned' for West Region a report showing the British workers joining the French at lunch. The Sud Aviation canteen, filled with a thousand enthusiastic eaters, contrasted vividly with BAC's austere counterpart at Bristol. The buffet line began with half-litre cartons of wine, which the British noticeably appreciated as much as the French. 'The Bristol men had no complaints about the food — except perhaps there's too much garlic. The menu

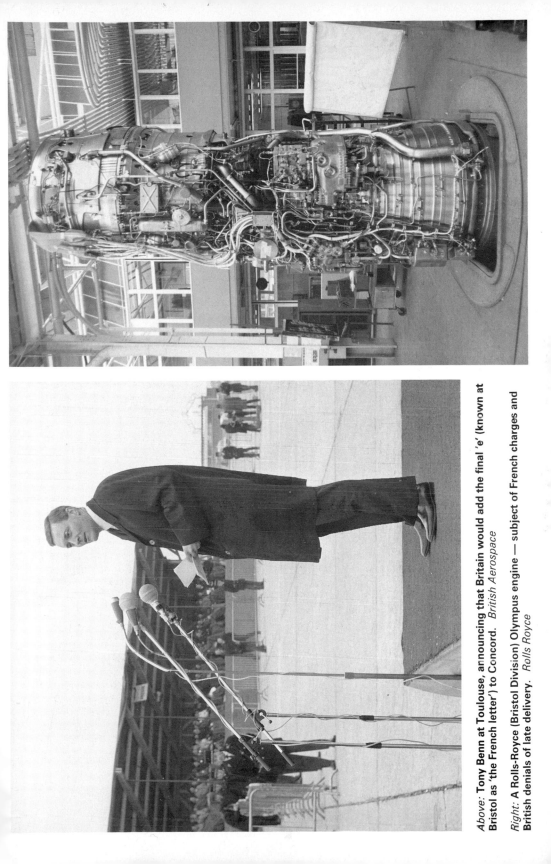

Above: **Tony Benn at Toulouse, announcing that Britain would add the final 'e' (known at Bristol as 'the French letter') to Concord.** *British Aerospace*

Right: **A Rolls-Royce (Bristol Division) Olympus engine — subject of French charges and British denials of late delivery.** *Rolls Royce*

we enjoyed included soup, leeks in oil, gelatine canard, beef stew, macaroni cheese and an orange. And you have it *all*.' I certainly could not have done my pieces to camera if I had consumed all that — and there were those who admitted that it was important to get the precision work done before lunch.

Making the most of the fact that their 001 prototype was to roll-out and fly long before Britain's, the French flew in 700 guests from the US, Britain and European capitals to witness the ceremony. Because the runway and apron were covered with black ice despite the fact that this region of France was reputed to be semi-tropical, there was some discussion as to whether the ceremony should be reversed to a 'roll-in', with Concorde standing outside and the guests protected inside the hangar. But with stands erected for guests, podia for speakers, and mobile platforms in place for the TV crews, it was decided instead to issue them with blankets, and to instal infra-red heaters beneath the most important of the guests.

The guests arrived in eight aircraft from Britain, and five Caravelles from Paris — all due to return the same day, to the guests' relief and the disgust of the Toulouse hotels. The runway was so icy that the Caravelle pilots used tail parachutes instead of wheelbrakes to halt their aircraft.

But the guests, the journalists, and most of all the flimsily clad air stewardesses from the 16 customer airlines, were made to earn the champagne and canapes waiting inside the closed hangar. Jean Chamant, French Minister of Transport, talked for an hour while the guests huddled in their blankets and the TV crew and I muttered despairingly as any hopes we had of flying the film back to London in time for the evening bulletins disappeared. Film transmission by land line was just becoming possible but was still prohibitively expensive; video and direct satellite transmission was still years away. Somewhere buried in his speech Chamant uttered one usable sentence: the first prototype we were about to see was as much British as French — though it was hard to believe amid the forest of tricolour flags with just one Union Jack submerged among them. Wedgwood Benn, Britain's Technology Minister, unpopular though he was because no one was sure whether he embraced the anti-Concorde Labour line, or whether he supported it on behalf of his Bristol constituents, redeemed the occasion for the newsmen. Not only was he mercifully short, but he scored some useful points off the French, bearing in mind that de Gaulle, at the height of his power, was repeatedly saying 'Non' to Britain's efforts to join the Common Market.

On only one point had Anglo-French co-operation been marred, said Benn, and he had finally decided to remove it. In future England, as well as France, would spell Concorde with a final 'e'. (This conveniently ignored the fact that BAC had spelt it that way all along in defiance of a Government decree insisting on the English spelling in their official references to it.) After all, said Benn, E stood for Excellence, for England and Europe, towards which Britain was moving; E also stood for Entry and Entente. Frozen faces broke into a ripple of rather embarrassed laughter.

After the national anthems — the Marseillaise played by a well-rehearsed RAF band flown over for the occasion, and God Save the Queen played by a noticeably under-rehearsed French band — the shivering guests sighed with relief as the hangar doors at last rolled open, and Concorde 001 was towed slowly out, gleaming in the coat of white reflective paint needed to counter the friction-heating of supersonic flight.

While the guests, almost at a run, replaced Concorde in the warm hangar and fell upon the champagne and smoked salmon, and newspaper reporters were thundering up the staircases to fight for the limited number of available phones, the ordeal of the TV crews continued. Carefully angled by the cameramen to show the words along the fuselage, we were doing our 'stand-uppers' in front of Concorde's nose. French TV were on the side displaying 'Sud Aviation — British Aircraft Corporation'; we favoured the other side: 'British Aircraft Corporation — Sud Aviation.'

The big issue was whether Concorde really would make its maiden flight in only two months' time on 28 February 1968 — the date which the French in particular had had posted up for several years. Richard Dixon, then ITN air/industrial correspondent, was convinced the aircraft was months behind schedule — and so, but to a lesser extent, was I. But I also knew from experience of other maiden flights that it was possible to make things look good by sending off an airframe on a first flight with practically nothing that mattered inside — effectively concealing the truth. The official spokesmen for the Governments and the makers, but most of all Charles Gardner of BAC, were vehement with their insistence that it was on time. In the end, I swallowed my suspicions because this was, after all, a flag-waving rather than a 'knocking' occasion and said: '...But after five years she's not only on time; she's probably increased her lead over America to five years.'

Some of the truth emerged six weeks before the maiden flight was due. Jean Chamant told aviation journalists in Paris that the flight would be delayed because Britain had so far delivered only two of the prototype's jet engines, and that the next two would be delayed for a few weeks. What was by now called the Bristol division of Rolls-Royce (Rolls having taken over Bristol Siddeley) hotly and instantly denied it. 'The Minister's statement must be based on a misunderstanding,' said Rolls — the closest they could get to calling it a lie. There were in fact already four engines at Toulouse, and I had seen them myself, installed in 001 when it was rolled out. They were the ground-test engines, and another four — the flight-test engines — were in final assembly and would be ready on time for delivery. For once I believed without reservation what the British were saying, and pointed out in radio and TV pieces that the French had not yet completed the installation in the prototype of the systems that would enable the ground-test engines to be run for the vibration checks and taxying trials that must precede the maiden flight.

Chamant's public excuse for the delays must have been for internal political reasons — and he did, I was told, subsequently withdraw the complaint about the engines only to substitute charges that British sub-contractors were late delivering power-controls and other systems. No doubt to this day most French people believe his story and not the British rebuttal. But it caused acute embarrassment to French engineers and technicians, who knew the facts and worked loyally and well with their British counterparts.

The Olympus engines were a particularly sensitive subject so far as Rolls and BAC were concerned, for they were also to have been used in the TSR2 strike aircraft, and during Concorde planning it was expected that much of their development cost would come out of Britain's defence budget. When the incoming Labour Government cancelled TSR2, Defence Secretary Denis Healey may well have understood how many millions of pounds and manhours of work would be saved to his defence budget and transferred to Concorde costs. But it is doubtful that Aviation Minister Roy Jenkins, who was party to the political decision not to allow TSR2 to be used as a supersonic test bed after its cancellation, had the slightest idea of the knock-on effect on the project for which his Ministry was responsible.

I concluded my lead story on TV News by saying: 'Whoever is to blame, it's now likely that Concorde's maiden flight won't take place until May. But both the French and British companies are emphasising that the plane will still go into service in 1971. So it's all the more unfortunate that earlier predictions that each country would blame the other for any delays have so soon turned out to be true.'

Concorde's maiden flight was in the end a whole year late, and it must have been known at the time of the roll-out that there was no hope of meeting the 28 February target. I found it hard to forgive and forget the lies we were told, and never again really trusted a public relations person, whether employed by a company or the Government.

A rare moment of amity. The Author, left, with Charles Gardner, BAC public relations chief, right.

CHAPTER THREE

Concorde Flies

At last, in August 1968, Concorde 001's taxying trials began at Blagnac. The spectacle of the Anglo-French supersonic aircraft at last moving under its own power rated as a big story.

I flew to Toulouse with a camera crew, and with excitement we filmed as the aircraft's graceful 148 tons moved along at little more than walking pace. It was much smaller and lighter than the planned production aircraft, but nobody mentioned that. We filmed the safety barrier, designed to catch 001 if Andre Turcat, as he worked up to 140mph, overestimated his braking power and ran off the end of the runway. I snatched interviews with Turcat — lofty, cool and laid back — and with Brian Trubshaw — short, thickset and laconic — who was no more than a long-suffering spectator; and with that in the can we rushed back to London, where I appeared breathless on early evening TV News to say we would be showing the film as soon as it was processed.

On these occasions I offered up my agnostic prayers, with little confidence, that in the hurry the film would not be ruined in the 'soup'. All too often it was, and one was aware of suspicion that it was almost certainly my fault rather than that of clumsy technicians, who always had alibis. This time all was well and I was able to speculate on whether the Soviet Tu-144, so similar in appearance and so obviously a copy that we all called it 'Concordski', would beat 001 to the maiden flight. Neither in France nor England could we get any real guidance as to when 001 would be ready. The Russians were much more forthcoming, announcing with confidence that their first flight would be before the end of the year, and that they planned their first commercial supersonic service between Moscow and Tokyo starting in March 1970.

Britain's planemakers, once they had got used to the idea that France's prototype would fly first, had nursed private plans to equalise things by providing the first public presentation of the flying prototype at the Farnborough Air Show in September that year.

Now that was missed, and the French were working confidently towards showing 001 at their own Paris Air Show the following June — thus strengthening the popular illusion that it was more French than Anglo-French.

We of the media all enjoyed the roll-out and the accompanying rows over Britain's Concorde, designated 002, when at last it came nine months after 001's first appearance. British Aircraft Corporation's public relations people gave us

September 1968: Roll-out of Britain's 002 prototype — 'a normal working day' said BAC. Tail markings are for vibration and flutter tests. *British Aerospace Airbus*

24 hours' notice to get to Filton, near Bristol, to record it emerging from the enormous hangar built 23 years earlier in the vain hope that it would be needed for a production line of luxury Bristol Brabazon airliners.

For 002's first appearance there were no banners, no speeches and definitely no champagne, I reported — only the wailing of the siren warning workers to keep clear as the huge power-operated doors rolled back. 'But 002 was watched, rather silently, by several thousand Filton workers; and BAC officials were unrepentant: "This is a normal working day", they said. And 002 is ready for work — the flight-test engines are all installed.'

We watched it towed two miles to the far side of the airfield, to be backed into the noise-suppressing assemblies for engine runs and pressure tests, during which the fuselage would be blown up like a balloon. Overhead, emphasising the 'normal working day', repeated passes were being made by the adapted Vulcan bomber already flight-testing the Olympus engine. I interviewed everybody available about the likely date of 001's maiden flight, got nowhere and speculated on mid-November. 'In the meantime, a battle is developing between Pan American, Air France and BOAC. All three want the prestige of taking the first supersonic passengers across the Atlantic. So all three, it's been arranged, will get two Concordes at exactly the same time. And about Christmas, 1971, one will beat the other with the first flight. But it's likely there'll only be seconds in it.'

The rows followed next day, when spokesmen for Wedgwood Benn, as we still called him, made it clear that he was furious that as Minister of Technology he had not been invited to the roll-out. A very big sales opportunity had been incompetently handled, it was hinted. Neither the Minister nor his office, not even Jim Hamilton, DG of the Anglo-French Concorde Committee, had been told. Benn was 'incandescent' we reported, when some official attempted to smooth things over by saying he had been unable to attend because of a previous engagement. He had been in Bristol until midnight, 10hr before the roll-out, and left for London then to attend a morning Concorde meeting in London. The failure to notify Benn or his staff could only be construed as a calculated snub by BAC for the Government that tried to cancel Concorde and for the Minister whose support for the project was regarded as dubious.

The international supersonic race dwindled in importance while I covered the Apollo 7 and 8 missions; but I was back in London in time to report on the triumphant Soviet announcement that the Tu-144, in fulfilment of their promises, had made a successful maiden flight on the last day of the year. Although we had only 36sec of Soviet-provided film, I was given two minutes of what was then the prime time TV News, lasting a mere 10min at 8.50pm:

'Russia has big things in mind for her supersonic airliner. Just as she's bulldozing for herself a larger share of the world's shipping, so she intends to claim a much larger share of the world's aviation markets with this plane...The first passenger flight, from Moscow to Japan, has already been announced for October 1970 — two years before Concorde can hope to make it...Already at Moscow Airport the supersonic terminal is nearly complete. They've even got the food planned: space-age stuff, based on what cosmonauts eat. For instance, caviare squeezed out of tubes. The Russians have already agreed on routes through India to Japan. In Europe every time Concorde gets a route you can be certain Russia will insist on a reciprocal route for the Tu-144 right alongside it.

49

Vulcan bomber, fitted with special pod for flight-testing a Concorde Olympus engine, flew overhead during the 002 roll-out. *Rolls Royce*

October 1968: After the roll-outs came rising cost announcements.

Concorde cost soars to £700m

D.Mail 8-10 68

THE COST of C... airliner, ha... total ...

... the Anglo-French supersonic ...00 million to a staggering new ...e increase is expected to be ...er of Technology, Mr Anthony ...d Benn.

By
ANGUS MacPHERSON
Air Correspondent

...to-set off ...paign to ...0-seater, ...liner.

...rde re- ...nt has ...from ...e of ...pro-

ready now for airlines until 1972 at least.

The British and French Governments have both agreed to advance over £120 million each to the Concorde firms British Aircraft Corporation and Sud-Aviation in France on top of the development bill.

This is to be treated as a loan to get Concordes rolling quickly off the production lines, and will bring the taxpayers' investment in Concorde to around £1,000 million.

The intention of the Governments is that the sum of nearly £300 million advanced to finance production should be repaid rapidly by a levy on all Concordes sold.

Revolt

...the money spent on ...pment of the aircraft is a ...t Government grant, with ...mises about repayment. ...th the cost rocketing, ...tish and French Trea- ...at the point o...

Concorde employs 27,000 U.K. workers

The Financial Times Friday March 8 1968

BY MICHAEL DONNE, AIR CORRESPONDENT

A total of 27,000 workers throughout Britain are now engaged on various aspects of the Concorde Anglo-French supersonic airliner, with around 323 sub-contractors involved besides the main contractors, British Aircraft Corporation and Rolls-Royce.

This fact emerges from an analysis of the impact of the Concorde programme on the U.K. economy, carried out by the Society of British Aerospace Companies.

The figure takes no account of the work on the project being carried out in France. There are probably about the same number are employed, so that Concorde now occupies well over 50,000 workers in the U.K. and French industries.

So far as the U.K. itself is concerned, the SBAC says that virtu-... every major town in Britain ... more factories contri... each in its ...

of new techniques and equipment to meet the special and often stringent requirements of building, testing and operating the Concorde; in establishing new commercial technical and licensing links between U.K. companies and their Continental counterparts; in opening new markets for British products and in speeding the miniaturisations and improved performance of aviation equipment.

Britain's share

...cost of the Concorde's ...development is £250m. ...being spent ... ...blish-

Security for industrial buildings

By Our Architectural ...ondent
...trial buildings ...but im-

'What about America's supersonic plane? They've switched from a swing-wing to a big 250-seater with a fixed wing. But they're still arguing about the cost — at least a thousand million pounds. The one thing certain to result at last in a go-ahead at top speed on a rival American SST is tonight's news from Russia.'

Preparations for Concorde 001's maiden flight were the subject of endless separate and joint meetings for BBC Radio and TV, followed by negotiations, usually abrasive when Charles Gardner was involved, with BAC. Charles and his opposite number — a retired and elusive French general — actually had my sympathy as they were battered by demands from the world's media for filming and photographic positions guaranteed to provide the perfect view of the take-off and landing.

With more rewarding things to do, I delegated the meetings to a TV sub-editor then attached to my office, but in the end had a despairing note from 'H.E.P. Tel', whoever he was, making it clear that it was 'absolutely essential' that I personally made 'very firm application' for all my needs in the matter of passes and technical equipment. In addition to a live TV outside broadcast, there was to be filming in monochrome and colour, and it was added: 'Reserve space for up to a dozen small tins of 16mm film for BBC TV News in any aircraft provided by BAC to fly photographers' material to London. If possible we would like this aircraft to land at Luton rather than Heathrow.'

There was also much hysteria about the official chase plane, because the BAC/Sud photographer was proposing to use a 35mm camera rather than a 16mm film camera, 'which will save hours for all the TV news organisations.' The media was uninterested in the fact that the main role of the chase plane was to get good film of 001's flight performance — especially in the event of anything going wrong.

World interest in the story was increased in the weeks before the flight by full-page advertisements taken in the *Guardian* and other newspapers by 'The Anti-Concorde Project'. Described as 'Under the Patronage of Baroness (Lady Mary) Stocks and Baroness Wootton of Abinger', it carried the names of nearly 500 distinguished academics, scientists and others who supported it — many of whom perhaps lived to regret their signatures. Richard Wiggs, mentioned earlier, was Convener and Organiser, and affiliated bodies included 'Association Nationale Anti-Bangs (ANAB-France)'. Supersonic airliners would cause widespread serious disturbance and much damage, readers were told. 'The evidence is incontrovertible that to many people the bangs are insupportable. This applies especially to certain categories of people — for example, musicians, surgeons, children, invalids.' Authentication of these claims was sought by quoting *The Economist* and *The Observer* as anti-Concorde supporters; in fact, not to support the Anti-Concorde Project, it was implied, was to be written off as a moron.

Freddie Laker joined in with anti-Concorde comments at this time, too, though he was in effect to eat his words later on both issues he raised. He was then supporting the British Aircraft Corporation's unsuccessful efforts to start a rival to the European Airbus called the BAC Three-Eleven; in an interview with me in Tenerife he scathingly dismissed both the Airbus and Concorde as 'silly aeroplanes'!

When at last Concorde was ready, a single phone call to a friendly member of Gardner's staff brought me seven passes — two for correspondents, one for a 'secretary' (my wife Margaret, who had a magical way of getting people who hated one another to work together), two cameramen, one sound engineer and one production assistant. Even in those days it was a modest team for all the live radio and TV coverage planned, but no doubt there were dozens of BBC engineers and technicians involved behind the scenes with ORTF, the then excellent French radio and TV organisation much missed since being ruthlessly broken up by the French Government. Like Italy's RAI, whenever I was in their territory ORTF would set up a circuit for me to the BBC without fuss or bother, knowing that the BBC would do the same thing for them when their need arose.

As usual, covering the story itself was straightforward — almost restful compared with the preparations for it. Life was made easier too because I had all the facilities usually provided for an outside-broadcast commentator — direct lines to Broadcasting House and TV Centre, and even, as soon as the flight was over, a 'unilateral' — a TV link via satellite over which I could do my own description 'in vision'. Margaret and I spent a pleasant week in Toulouse, staying as usual at Le Bristol, and keeping well away from the Comtes des Toulouse Hotel, a new international skyscraper, housing the 'secretariat and joint information centre' consisting of BAC and Sud officials warring with as many of the hundreds of newsmen and TV crews from all over the world who could cram themselves in. Charles Gardner set the tone in his Press handout stating that the secretariat 'will NOT repeat NOT be in on the business of running a series of forecasts on the first flight date'.

Some final taxi runs, with Jean Franchi, described as 'substitute pilot', at the controls, provided two days of scene-setting stories. He took 001 up to take-off speed, and must have been sorely tempted to lift-off. Afterwards the aircraft was taken back to the hangar for what we called 'press-ups' — lowering and raising the undercarriage 30 times to ensure that it would not jam. This, however, was not necessary for the brief maiden flight, when it was not intended to retract the undercarriage anyway. Then came two days of bad weather and capricious winds, and for a story I fell back on local speculation that if Turcat did not make the flight before the Friday, the last day of February, and exactly one year to the day after it should have flown, the attempt would have to be postponed until the following Monday. The 1,500 gendarmes who had thrown a cordon around the area, barring everyone from entry except those of us privileged to adorn our cars with elaborate passes, would have too big a problem keeping out the public, said the local wiseacres. They were quite wrong.

All day Saturday Concorde 001 sat on the runway, fully checked out, with 25 tons of fuel on board — twice the quantity needed for the first flight. Fog and heavy cloud depressed everyone from Turcat to the camera crews. For once no one in the Toulouse area lingered over lunch. The fog cleared first, then the heavy cloud broke. The chase planes took off to send back visibility reports. Soon after 3pm Turcat tentatively started one engine, the cameras started rolling, there were frantic calls by the news engineers to open up the outside broadcast lines — and Turcat shut down the engine. Thirty minutes later, all four Rolls-Royce Olympus jets burst into life, 001's needle-nose was drooped so that the pilots could see over and beyond it, the engine afterburners banged into life. Propelled by the 60-ton thrust provided by the flaming, smoking and crackling engines, Concorde was on its way. 'She was airborne at 3.38. From standing start to lift-off at 200mph took only 20sec. A steep climb to 7,500ft, and for half an hour Turcat varied the speed and height and practised turns.

Model of one of the two 200-ton noise-suppressor assemblies used at BAC Filton and RAF Fairford for airfield ground-runs of the 38,050lb thrust engines. *Capper Neill News*

Left: **2 March 1969: Andre Turcat going through his checklist before the take-off (an autographed picture).** *de Coninck*

Below left: **The world's press — including Raymond Baxter for BBC TV — check their communications.** *de Coninck*

Right: **Sir George Edwards, head of BAC, shelters from the cold beneath his famous pork pie hat.** *de Coninck*

Below: **'She Flies' at last.**

Right: **Photo of TV screen of Concorde flying with caption 'Reginald Turnill from Toulouse'.** *Unknown viewer*

Right: **The Author describing the maiden flight for TV News.** *de Cornick*

Below: **Certificates were awarded just for being present at 001's maiden flight.**

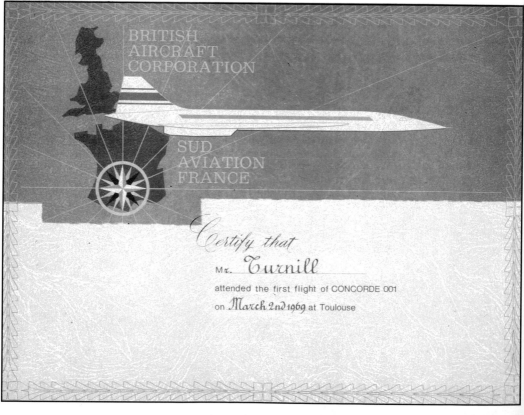

BRITISH
AIRCRAFT
CORPORATION

SUD
AVIATION
FRANCE

Certify that

Mr. *Turnill*

attended the first flight of CONCORDE 001

on *March 2nd 1969* at Toulouse

'Two chase planes — a British Meteor and a French Paris — filmed him all the way, the French plane providing live TV coverage most of the time. Because of the wind and deteriorating weather, Turcat decided not to make a practice approach. Instead, he came straight in. A perfect touchdown, with reverse thrust and braking parachute.'

Someone, somewhere, took an excellent photograph of Concorde off his TV screen as my report went out, captioned at the bottom 'REGINALD TURNILL FROM TOULOUSE' and with the extraordinary mental aberration often displayed by members of the public, sent it to Raymond Baxter. The viewer was convinced that my friend and colleague Raymond was doing the report, despite my name in half-inch letters. His confusion was understandable, since Raymond sat beside me doing the live commentary for TV, while I did the commentary for radio. But then I did the report for the TV News bulletins down the still open satellite line Baxter had been using. The News Division insisted that their own correspondents contributed the news reports — mainly because outside broadcast commentators necessarily talked around the subject, and did not provide tightly-worded reports to the required length. But in due course Raymond, always an easy man to work with, passed the photo on to me, and I have displayed it proudly ever since — the only physical proof of my work that day, since videos were still a long way ahead.

As the four-man French crew came down the aircraft steps — there were no British aboard, explained BAC rather sourly, because it was not wise to use both the Anglo-French test pilots on what was inevitably a risky occasion, and it was also better to work in only one language — Henri Ziegler and George Edwards, as heads of Sud Aviation and BAC, rushed to greet them. Now that it had flown, they were confident that the politicians would find it almost impossible to cancel Concorde.

With sweat gleaming on his great bald dome, Turcat happily presented his team to the jostling media in the airport conference hall. 'It flies pretty well,' he said; and in a reference to the long delay before it had done so: 'It justifies our methods. But we've got years and months of work ahead before it's ready for passenger service.'

Five weeks later, with nine flights behind him, but with supersonic speed still to be reached, it was Andre Turcat's turn to be a mere spectator. Brian Trubshaw ('Trubby' to every BAC worker, an affectionate diminutive definitely not used in his hearing), took the limelight. He had accompanied Turcat on one of the French flights; and now Britain's Concorde 002 was ready for its first take-off from Filton, near Bristol. Turcat had had lots of trouble with the weather; Trubshaw was to contend with some serious technical hitches.

We of the media had different problems. Once 002 had taken off from Filton it was to land 50 miles away at RAF Fairford in Gloucestershire, never to return. That was because Trubshaw, supported by his second-in-command, John Cochrane, had decreed that the length and state of the Filton runway was unsuitable for the flight test programme. Brian himself said that his decision did 'not go down at all well' — which was not surprising, because switching the work to Fairford must have added untold millions to development costs. There were protracted arguments with Concorde's designers, who were supported by the French in their desire to get the Filton runway accepted as suitable for the test programme. But Trubshaw remained adamant, and I sometimes wondered whether BAC ever considered the alternative of changing the chief test pilot to one who would accept the Filton conditions — but of course any subsequent accident could then have been blamed on such a decision.

The media for quite different reasons shared the initial unhappiness of the Fairford villagers, who soon became proud of their Concorde links. Royal Aircraft Establishment acoustics experts successfully reassured local residents by bringing their most sensitive test equipment from Farnborough to transform the 15th century parish church into a temporary aerospace test centre. That was to prove that vibrations from Concorde's take-off and landing noise would not damage the 28 unique stained glass windows, dating back to 1490.

The vibrations from the church organ were potentially much more lethal than Concorde would be, concluded RAE's Head of Acoustics. It was a measure of the resentment of Fairford in those pre-flight days that while I was covering this story, and parked for lunch outside the village pub, the local bobby sneaked along, checked that my road tax licence appeared to be a few days out of date, and had me summonsed — without bothering to check that I was in fact awaiting the arrival of my paid tax disc.

For 002's maiden flight two helicopters had been laid on for the Minister of Technology and Andre Turcat, so that they could chase Concorde 002 from Filton to Fairford; but there was no way I could get to Fairford in time for the landing after doing live descriptions of the take-off. For once, BAC came to the rescue. I had done a nostalgic broadcast on 'Today' entitled 'Give Me Apollo Every Time', pointing out that while NASA deluged the media with information, on both the Concorde maiden flights the only way I got hold of a full Press Kit was by stealing one when no one was looking! My need, I considered, was more pressing than anyone else's. But now, fearing a skyfull of helicopters chartered by the media stampeding between Filton and Fairford, BAC announced that the Concorde crews, having deposited 002 safely at Fairford, would use the helicopters to fly back to us at Filton for a news conference — promising, on their honour, not to allow any newsman at Fairford to approach them!

It was a long day when 002 took to the air on 9 April 1969 — but for once my part of it all worked well. In addition to the Anti-Concorde Project, the big US planemakers were increasingly apprehensive because, while their proposed SST was neither designed nor funded, Concorde actually existed as a practical proposition. So again there were live inserts into the main radio and TV news programmes, and I had to do them all. Happily there was no morning TV, so I could do my progress reports live into 'Today' at 7.15 and 8.15, be interviewed by Jimmy Young at 11.25, report again in the 1pm news, describe the take-off as it happened at 2.20pm into Radios 1 & 2, followed by interviews into the 6pm News and 'Newstime' at 7.30 (which had just replaced Radio Newsreel), plus TV pieces on BBC1 at 5.50 and 8.50 and a long roundup on BBC2 at 7.30. I was still being interviewed into the 11pm Radio 4 news, and by then I was a talking zombie, answering questions as required, and leaving it to Margaret and the office to arrange pre-recordings just before transmission when the commitments clashed.

As always the disadvantage of all this was that unlike the newspaper correspondents I had no time to talk to my contacts about what was not being revealed in the Press handouts. As it happened, we all missed the best stories to

The essence of Concorde is speed. BAC/Aerospatiale believe that the resulting time savings, which in most cases are more than 50%, will be highly attractive to the First Class and business passengers.

ROUTE	CURRENT JOURNEY TIME Hrs : Mins.	CONCORDE JOURNEY TIME Hrs : Mins.	TIME SAVING %
New York — Buenos Aires	16 : 50	7 : 20	56
— Lima	9 : 15	3 : 43	60
— Panama City	6 : 15	2 : 27	61
— Rio de Janeiro	13 : 55	7 : 16	48
— Santiago	14 : 30	6 : 19	56
Los Angeles — Lima	8 : 12	3 : 59	51
Miami — Lima	6 : 20	3 : 01	52

Top: **Chart of Configuration Developments issued at the time of the first flight. (Carries BAC identity).**

Above: **Concorde Time Savings Chart.** *BAC/Aerospatiale*

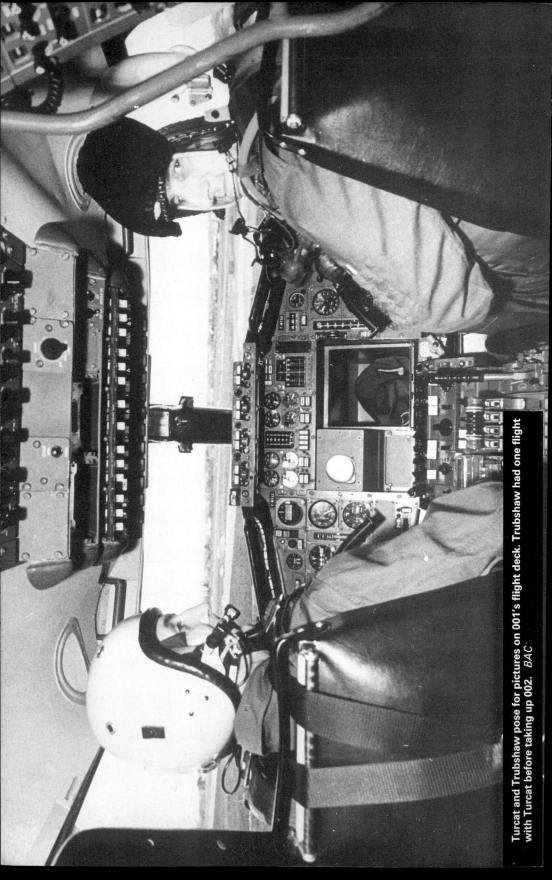

Turcat and Trubshaw pose for pictures on 001's flight deck. Trubshaw had one flight with Turcat before taking up 002. *BAC*

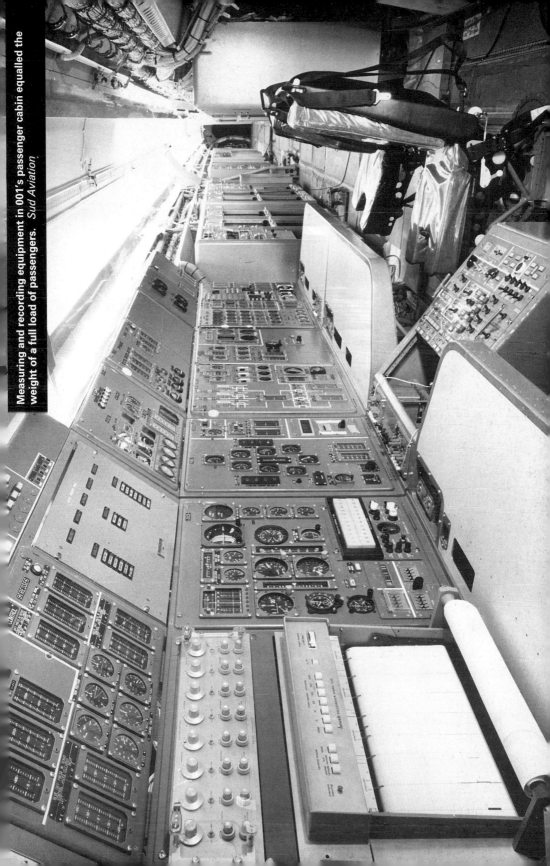

Measuring and recording equipment in 001's passenger cabin equalled the weight of a full load of passengers. *Sud Aviation.*

come out of the maiden flight — details of which I did not learn until long afterwards.

Brian Watts, the flight engineer and third member of the flight deck crew — there were in fact three more, seldom mentioned engineers monitoring the flight test equipment in the main cabin — rang his mother on the morning of the maiden flight to wish her a happy birthday. 'Are you doing anything today?' she asked.

'Not a lot. I'm going in to work in a moment,' he said, anxious not to cause her any alarm. In fact his wife was going in too, in the hope of witnessing the first take-off. We all knew by then that Concorde's prototype Olympus engines were noisy and dirty, emitting what Trubshaw described as 'a great cloud of unburnt fuel sitting behind the aeroplane', but this was new to the wives. 'We got the engines running at take-off power for several seconds before we even selected reheat. Then we cooked them up a bit at take-off power, and only then did we take the brakes off.' The volume of noise on that occasion was so unexpected that Mrs Watts fainted, and did not come round until after 002 had taken off.

On the flight deck both Cochrane and Watts were equally taken aback and during the short flight wondered whether they could tolerate it during the whole test programme. But the reason for it so far as they were concerned was that, for safety reasons, the maiden flight was made with both the nose and the metal visor down, as well as the undercarriage. The aircraft's speed was also kept down to 250kt. 'Some flights later,' said Cochrane, 'when we pulled the visor up for the first time I thought all the engines had stopped because we then had a very quiet flight deck.'

The visor arrangement, which can still be seen on 002 on display in the Science Museum at Yeovilton, Somerset, was the second cause of friction between the test pilots and Concorde's designers.

'Most of the visor was metal, and you just had two little peepholes to see through,' said Trubshaw, 'and we were convinced that one day this lot would jam up when we came in to land, and we always felt that at best we would get two marks for a nice try! There were various ideas for television screens and things like that; but in the end, and under pressure from outside parties as well, the visor was made transparent as it is on all the aeroplanes in service today.'

The major crisis on the maiden flight, of which we media watchers, dependent by then on a TV picture relayed from Fairford were completely unaware, came as 002 was approaching Fairford for its landing, when Brian Trubshaw reported that both radio altimeters had failed. But there was high tension in the Fairford Flight Test Centre as they watched a perfect, if rather 'positive' landing, followed by release of the braking parachute. An undisturbed Trubshaw had had to face bigger crises during his days as an RAF bomber captain. Long afterwards Brian Trubshaw explained what happened at the end of what he had thought was going to be a trouble-free flight:

'As soon as we had made our first approach and got lined up we realised we had hit one problem. Because in an aeroplane of this sort you land in a very high nose-up attitude, we use radio altimeters which provide a very accurate measurement of your height above the ground for judging the last part of the approach and landing. The co-pilot was to call out the heights as we came down, and particularly the heights from 100 ft down. When they both failed

62

above: **April 1969: 002's first lift-off from Filton.** *de Coninck*

below: **Trubshaw did not mention the failed radio altimeters when I interviewed him after the maiden flight.** *de Coninck*

there wasn't a damn thing we could do about it, so we were faced with what you might call 'eyeballing' the first landing at Fairford without this very valuable information — with which incidentally we'd done all our practising. It's not easy with a high-sitting aeroplane like Concorde; for the landing judgement it's quite crucial to know what the wheel height is. We probably arrived on the ground about a second before we thought we were going to. I wouldn't say it was a very heavy landing, but it was a firm landing and that was that.'

I would have heard about this brief drama much sooner if, instead of having to rush back to London for the late TV news, I had been able to accept Brian's invitation at the end of the filmed interview after the flight, to join the triumphant crew at the subsequent celebrations. Sheila Scott, famous for her solo flights in light aircraft had made a huge gooey cake for the occasion; and in the Directors' Mess there were presents: a silver salver and silver cigarette lighters for the crew, and large bouquets for wives and girlfriends. 'After that,' said Brian, 'we followed what has always been traditional after a maiden flight. We went out to the local pubs with all the chaps who had actually built the aeroplane. There were a lot of them, not only from BAC but from Rolls-Royce and all the other companies — far too many for one pub. In fact there were about four very good parties going on — and fortunately the breathalyser didn't work in those days.'

Next day, when I might have filled in more details of the first flight drama, media interest had already switched to other subjects; in my field the emphasis was on Technology Minister Wedgwood Benn's talks with French and German ministers, who wanted to know whether Britain, as a mark of gratitude for all their Concorde co-operation, would join with them in building a European Airbus.

Britain's pre-production prototype 01 shown with the transparent visor demanded by Trubshaw to provide better landing visibility. *de Coninck*

CHAPTER FOUR

Supersonic Concorde

Striving to keep ahead in the supersonic race, the Russians announced on 5 June 1969 that the Tu-144 had become the first commercial transport to exceed Mach 1.

It was not until October, six months after 002 had first flown, that Andre Turcat took 001 through the sound barrier.

That same month the US Government decided to back Boeing's supersonic project with a £1,800 millions loan, and their first flight was targeted for 1972. Alarmed by that, the Boulton Paul, Rolls Royce and other British technicians at Toulouse thought that Concorde flight testing was all much too slow, and complained that 'Dad', as they called Turcat, insisted on doing everything by the book. But Turcat, as I pointed out in my story about his brief few minutes at M1.05 — less than 700mph, and his height of nine miles causing no sonic bang — had to check the correct operation of the complex fuel transfer system needed to prevent the nose dropping as supersonic speed caused the aircraft's centre of gravity to move. City Editors were frequently 'fed' stories, almost always untrue, that technical troubles were escalating Concorde costs, but there was never a story about fuel transfer — no doubt because few people had the slightest understanding of the requirement.

Even less understood at that time, because we were not told (for good commercial reasons, for once), was the still more critical trial-and-error development of the engine intake and exhaust nozzles. These too had to adjust themselves automatically to the aircraft's speed, because, for instance, when the incoming air was being rammed in at twice the speed of sound, the shaped surface of the 14ft engine intake had to reduce its speed by 1,000mph to Mach 0.5 before it reached the engine. This business of working out the correct variable geometry — a technical problem that the Russians never completely solved — for both the intake and exhaust nozzles, and adding the thrust-reversal capability to the latter, could not be done in ground-based test chambers.

Three completely different designs were needed between the first flight of the prototype and the production Concorde to achieve a successful combination. Although I did not understand these details at the time, this was exactly the sort of advanced technology, with its spin-off in many different directions, which always convinced me that Concorde was the sort of project in which Britain needed to be involved if she were to stay at the leading edge.

These problems explain why it was Turcat's task to increase 001's speed so gradually and painstakingly to a modest M1.3, or 800mph, for longer and longer durations, and why at that stage the first prototype was grounded for a more advanced flight control system to be fitted. Then Brian Trubshaw was to use 002 for Phase Four of the development programme, taking his aircraft up to the planned cruising speed of Mach 2, or about 1,400mph. Turcat made good use of some of those gentle early flights to foster good relations with the airlines by giving pilots of the main airline customers — BOAC, Air France, PanAm, and TWA, a spell at the controls of 001. It was a shrewd move, because they were all won over by its handling qualities — and it helped too to establish France as leader of the project.

I fitted in brief stories about all this between covering the first Apollo missions, and especially the first two moonlandings in 1969. Jim Hamilton and Ministry of Technology officials looked ahead and worried about the supersonic test route which 002 would need, which we had tended to assume would be out of sight and sound, far out at sea. Not so. It had to be near enough to UK land bases for its performance to be kept under continuous radar surveillance — and in case of accident the flights must not be over deep water, so that the wreckage could be quickly recovered. Also, the route must always be near enough to the coastline for helicopters to rescue the crew.

France, it seemed had no problem; the Bay of Biscay met their needs. In Britain's case however the requirements played right into the hands of the anti-Concorde groups. The East Coast was ruled out, I reported in solemn analyses on BBC2, because Trubshaw would finish his run over densely populated Holland and Belgium. The only possibility was to start his Mach 2 runs over Northern Scotland at Cape Wrath, passing over the Western Isles, skimming the coasts of Northern Ireland on one side and the Isle of Man on the other, just missing Anglesey, but inescapably passing over Pembroke and Cornwall. Then 002 could be throttled down, and turn back to land at Fairford.

Before the first such run, five countries, led by Sweden, whose population had been much alarmed by Bo Lundberg's dire predictions, decided on protective action by announcing that they would be banning supersonic flights over their territory. The others were Norway, Holland, West Germany and Switzerland. Britain and France were more concerned about Boeing's success in getting orders for the new 747 Jumbo Jet. The airlines were investing so heavily in that that doubts were being raised as to whether there would be sufficient money left to buy Concordes when at last they became available.

It was April 1970 when Brian Trubshaw started his runs down the West Coast route, with new flying controls and — 'a unique feature', I pointed out — automatically-controlled air intakes.

A less publicised feature was a new type of accident recorder, with 300 channels recording technical data and five others for recording the voices of the pilots and technicians. As the data was gathered it was simultaneously transmitted to recording equipment on the ground, so that if anything went wrong during prototype flight tests, a complete picture would be available.

At Fairford I watched 002 take off making a great deal of smoke, and passed on to the public BAC's explanation that the aircraft had just been fitted with supersonic flight development engines, and that when it went into passenger

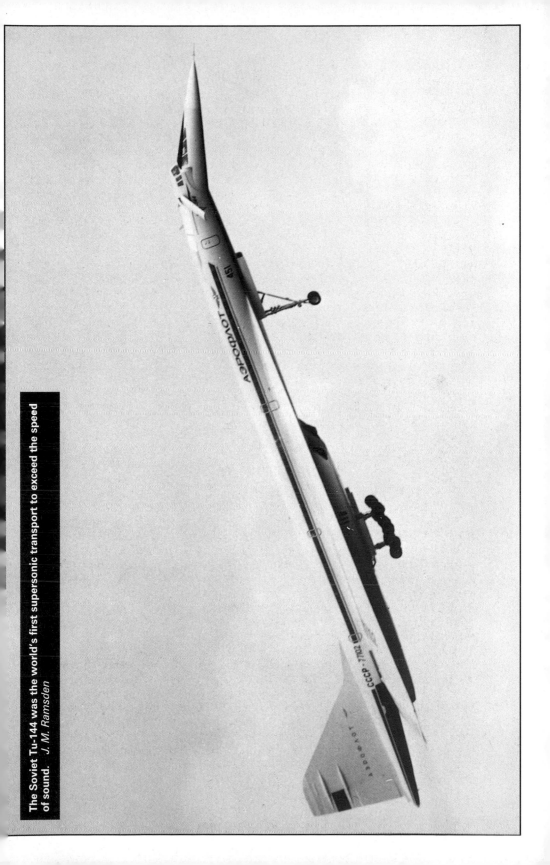

The Soviet Tu-144 was the world's first supersonic transport to exceed the speed of sound. *J. M. Ramsden*

Left: **Capt Paul Roitch of Pan American, left centre, and Capt Henderson of United, right centre, flanked by Turcat and Trubshaw after flying Concorde. Their hopes that their airlines would buy Concorde were not fulfilled.** *Sud Aviation*

Below: **Mr Tommy Frost, Rolls-Royce test pilot, left centre, with Capt Al White former B70 test pilot, in TWA Captain's uniform, right centre, another Concorde enthusiast who was to be disappointed.**

service the fuel would be vaporised before it was burned, 'so there should be no smoke at all'.

But just before he made his first sustained supersonic run, with Welsh indignation mounting over the threat to St David's Cathedral in Pembrokeshire, and Cornish anger being voiced over the threat to Truro Cathedral, there was a new sensation.

On the day in August when, but for bad weather, Trubshaw would have topped 1,000mph for the first time, a US Congressional report was issued claiming that the Anglo-French Concorde would be a commercial flop, and that because it would not find much of a market anyway, there was no need for a rival US SST. It generated much anger on both sides of the Atlantic for different reasons. The US aviation industry was horrified at the suggestion that they should abandon the supersonic race, and two of the ten Senators involved dissociated themselves from the report, and a third issued a scathing rebuttal. The US airlines had all refused to give evidence, and no one from Britain or France had been asked to give evidence or provide any information. What the Committee had done — and its chairman was Senator William Proxmire of Wisconsin, one of the few States with no stake in aerospace — was to invite Mary Goldring, of *The Economist*, well-known scourge of British aviation and avowed opponent of Concorde, to fly to Washington and give evidence against it — all expenses paid by Congress. I did not share Mary's views, but she was a well-liked and respected member of the group of British aerospace journalists who often found themselves travelling the world together. Now those newspapers which happened to be pro-Concorde at the time — they tended to follow the fashion so far as that was concerned — virtually accused her of treason. I summoned her to the BBC TV News studio for an interview — and was surprised and impressed when she came. Alas, I have no record of what she said, but I remember getting spirited replies to my questions.

Political erosion of President Nixon's support for America's supersonic plane was even more sustained and intense than the opposition to Concorde in Britain, and there was general relief in the aviation business when, in May 1970, the Russians announced that they had achieved twice the speed of sound in the Tu-144 — and this despite problems with very high fuel consumption. Poor Trubshaw found himself grounded for weeks by strikes and overtime bans by BAC workers. Against that, however, the British Government, desperately trying to curry favour with both sides, announced that it was planning legislation to ban supersonic flights over Britain — a decision which was to have unfortunate and far-reaching effects a few years later when Britain vainly sought permission from Malaysia and other countries for supersonic overflights of their lightly populated areas.

Just before Trubshaw actually did start down 'Boom Alley' in late August, I enjoyed myself in a broadcast entitled 'A Slight Attack of the Concorde Horrors':

'This project seems to bring out the worst in everybody'. The professional objectors have excelled themselves from the start.

'We've had maps of the world looking like balls of string, they're so wrapped around with the boom or doom carpets they're convinced that supersonic aircraft will make. On the ground, all our ancient monuments are going to fall down as Concorde passes overhead, though neither human beings nor modern churches appear, in their minds, to be in hazard. In the air, the aircraft's fuel, heated by skin friction, will burst into flames; and the very latest nightmare is that, failing all these other things, Concorde's passage through the upper atmosphere will dissipate the ozone, allowing ultraviolet radiation to heat up the earth's surface. There are times when I for one would welcome such a development in Britain; but two scientific groups in America have just concluded that this problem, like the others, "probably does not exist"...One's fellow journalists are particularly liable to attacks of the Concorde horrors...If it is going to happen, everybody wants to go down in history as being first with the "Concorde Cancelled" story.

'The real trouble with this project has nothing to do with the aircraft itself. It just happens to be plumb in the centre of all our worries about the future: whether we can possibly make a success of working so closely with continental countries if we join the Common Market...whether we're big enough, financially or technically, to tackle such grand projects at all — or whether, on the other hand we shall die as a nation if we DON'T embark on such gambles.'

I had the feeling, I said, that come 1974, we should find that Concorde was in routine airline service, that it was just another aeroplane, and that was that. This sort of broadcast brought me little praise inside or outside the BBC — it was too prosaic altogether, and undermined the drama of the horror stories so enjoyed not only by the newspapers but by BBC radio and TV programmes like The World at One and Panorama. On the news programmes my attitude was received with disappointed resignation.

At last, as August ended, the Ministry of Technology gave the promised 24-hours' advance warning that the booms were about to start. Ministry officials, university research teams and countless thousands of holidaymakers took up positions at points along the route from Sutherland in Northern Scotland, to Pembroke in Wales, where, with a TV crew, I joined Jim Hamilton and Dai Webb, who was an acoustics expert from Farnborough. He thoroughly enjoyed briefing the world's press: in the prevailing weather conditions, he said, the boom would be as sharp and loud as it was ever likely to be — two crisp and distinct bangs — and those who heard them would never again confuse the bang made by a supersonic airliner with the more thunderlike rumble made by supersonic fighter planes. However, he added, a thousand Concorde bangs would not move the windows of St David's Cathedral as much as the routine temperature difference between night and day.

I watched the TV sound recordist anxiously turn down his recording equipment, for fear that it would be overloaded by the intensity of the boom, and he would get nothing. The first boom over Oban, at 5.45pm, was reported over the intercom; Concorde swept on, at over 1,100mph, eight miles high. Tensely, 20min later, we saw a pencil-white contrail approaching St David's Head. Then, a gentle 'Pop-pop'. Was that it?

Trubshaw had apparently been slightly off course, and, we were assured, people much further inland had heard the sharp 'crack-crack' promised by Dai Webb. And, with a faulty instrument wrongly warning that an engine was overheating, Trubshaw was obliged to land 002 on three engines. Red lights on 002's dashboard had a way of appearing at much more inconvenient times than on Turcat's 001!

For once BAC agreed that public appearances at the Farnborough Air Show were of more importance than a few days' delay in test flights, and Trubshaw's low passes over the runway showing the pure, beautiful lines of his aircraft were an emotional, tear-jerking occasion. On the final Sunday, with 100,000 members of the public enduring torrential rain, Brian Trubshaw took off from Fairford determined not to disappoint them even though the weather was closing in and he knew he might not be able to return there. After three low-level passes he had to divert to Heathrow for the supersonic aircraft's first landing at a civil airport. It was accompanied by a shattering roar from the almost unsilenced flight development engines, quite frightening to those not expecting it. Floods of protests followed, and the British Airports Authority expressed regret for the disturbance — 'quite untypical of what Concorde will be like in passenger service'. But the Anti-Concorde Project was to make good use of the incident.

Still maintaining its narrow lead, the Tu-144 claimed for the record book on 26 May 1970 the first flight by a commercial transport to exceed Mach 2 — though its designer Alexei Tupolev admitted it was only 'for several minutes'.

Trubshaw and Turcat, now five months behind, made a pact that they would both achieve Mach 2 on the same day. That was 4 November 1970, and Trubshaw should in fact have been a few hours ahead in passing this significant development milestone. But before achieving it Trubshaw had another of those dashboard lights warning that his No.4 engine was overheating, and had to turn back. Turcat of course had no such problems and flew for 53min at 1,320mph.

'Despite disappointment about Britain's Concorde having to turn back, jubilation tonight in both France and Britain,' I reported on TV News. '. . . Concorde is now virtually certain to go into production.'

The 'jubilation' I reported was less than the whole truth, Aerospatiale and BAC having conspired to conceal from us that while Concorde had had no trouble in reaching its design speed, terrifying problems were encountered when the time came to slow down. John Cochrane put it this way: 'It was relatively easy to get to Mach 2; the trouble was to slow down again without getting into what bore a strong resemblance to being in a train wreck. Believe me, it was not funny at all; not only did it sound like a bomb going off, it shook the aeroplane about something fierce!'

Brian Trubshaw described how, after rounding the north of Scotland in 002 they reached Mach 2 for the first time flying south down 'Bomb Alley':

'We were doing beautifully, and I always remember saying 'I think that's enough; just throttle them back gently, please John' — and as he touched the throttles I felt World War 3 had started. There were some of the biggest explosions outside we had ever heard. We actually had both the right-hand engines surging. Of course we became great experts on it in due time; but to be confronted with this the first time was a bit unusual, to say the least. So anyway we cut the flight short at that stage and went back to Fairford.'

The surging has been described by one of the programme directors on the Olympus engine as 'a sort of hiccup or forward-firing "backfire" caused by a sudden breakdown of the airflow in the engine'. If not corrected, the engine would go into a cyclic surge condition like a quick-firing Bofors gun. 'That, I think it would be fair to say, identified the one big technical obstacle that had to be overcome on this aeroplane — to make the whole of the powerplant system work,' explained Trubshaw.

'We embarked on an enormous programme of intake development, and a very great deal of it John did on the pre-production aeroplane; but it was carried

Above: **Jan 1972: 002, diverted to Heathrow by bad weather, appears to have taken a wrong turn and meets a jumbo jet.** *de Coninck*

Below: **November 1970: Turcat reached Mach 2 for the first time. Trubshaw soon followed, and here 002's instruments show a speed of Mach 2.04 at an altitude of 52,700ft.** *de Coninck*

on right through the pre-production and production planes before we got one which was, you might say, compatible with roast beef and champagne in the back. Because the prototypes were very marginal in this engine surging, we were fortunate that on them we had speed brakes on the rear of the fuselage. We were able to put the speed brakes out, and decelerate to about Mach 1.7, and never throttled the engines until we got back to that. The only way you got away with throttling the engines on the prototype was to bang them shut —what you call a slam deceleration, and then the engines didn't surge. That was the start of a programme which covered hundreds of deliberate engine surges.

'The first major inflight incident occurred on the French prototype following an engine surge when a large part of the intake system was spat out in front of the engine and then went into its neighbour, so that the aeroplane finished up on two engines out over the water.'

A few days after 002 had achieved Mach 2 for the first time I was within half an hour of breaking what I was confident was a small 'scoop'. I was invited to take breakfast in his hotel with Floyd Hall, president of Eastern Airlines, then the world's second biggest airline, when he visited London, and he told me that his would be the first of the 16 airlines then holding 72 'options' on Concordes to convert them into firm orders. He gave me the routes on which he planned to operate — London-New York-New Orleans and Mexico City, and presented me with a splendid Concorde model painted in Eastern livery. The airline would have to put down £12 millions — £2 millions per plane — to convert their six options into orders, I pointed out. Perhaps it was this that alarmed his Board members. With my script complete, for once on the teleprompter in good time, and the model standing on the desk from which I would deliver my report, his public relations man rang to say that Hall 'must have stumbled over his words', and if we used the story they would have to deny it.

In the US, where the House of Representatives had approved the Government's plan to fund the rival Boeing SST, the year ended with dismay when the Senate, influenced by environmental arguments, turned against it. The world's major airlines had shown far more confidence in the ultimate production of a US SST than in Concorde, with the result that 26 airlines — mostly the same ones that had taken options on Concorde — had also given Boeing provisional orders for a total of 122. They heard the news with a mixture of relief and disbelief that Europe could continue with something that the US had abandoned. At first sight, abandonment of its US competitor could add another 100 to Concorde's expected order book of 250, I reported; but the truth was that Anglo-French salesman were much alarmed at the prospect of the competition being killed. As they feared, the British and French Governments reacted by delaying yet again the decision to provide funds for full Concorde production.

By January 1971 the Concorde prototypes had together logged 100 supersonic flights. But although the test flight programme was going remarkably well, there was still little confidence that the project could survive. Rolls Royce were bankrupted by development problems with the RB211 jet engine, and although this was for the future widebody subsonic aircraft, and the competence of Concorde's Olympus engines was not in question, it added to the general uncertainty. Brian Trubshaw was persuaded to take time off test-flying to hold news conferences at which he did his best to persuade the world's airlines that

73

Concordes would improve their overall profitability by 3%. Efforts were made to arrange a grand signing ceremony by BOAC, Air France and Australia's Qantas airline at the forthcoming Paris Air Show. By then, it was hoped, the American airlines would have forgiven and forgotten the troubles involving Rolls, Lockheed and the Tristar aircraft, and be convinced that, no matter what reservations they had, they could not afford *not* to order Concordes.

There was much hard bargaining between the French and British Governments, BOAC and Air France, about Concorde's selling price.

With the Treasury on their back, British ministers now thought that the airlines should be charged about £13 millions per aircraft with spare parts. That would enable them to recover at least a small proportion of development costs — by that time expected to be £800 millions. The French took the practical view that it was no good jeopardising sales prospects just to get back a tiny fraction of development costs, and urged that the charge should be kept down to £10 millions per plane, plus £2 millions for spares. One Sunday *The Observer,* as part of its dedicated anti-Concorde campaign, led with a story that BOAC had told the Government it could see no way of operating the aircraft economically. This story, which was not directly denied by Keith Granville, by then BOAC's chairman, reinforced American airlines' doubts, and probably started the chain of events that finally destroyed Concorde's sales prospects.

That Sunday was a thin day for news, and I was woken at 1am from a deep sleep. I slid out of bed, drove from Sydenham to Broadcasting House, woke a few senior airline people in my turn, recorded a piece which led the BBC early morning news bulletins, drove back home and slid quietly back into bed beside Margaret. When I switched on the bedside radio in the morning she was astonished to hear my voicepiece. She too had slept soundly, and had no idea that I had been absent from the marital bed for several hours. What was behind BOAC's leaked report to the Government (*The Observer'*s report was 'an over-simplification' I was assured) was their own long-term policy aimed at getting a Government subsidy to operate the aircraft. This was to safeguard the profitability of their operations even if it was at the expense of destroying the British Aircraft Corporation's sales campaign.

But the 'leaking' of the BOAC document, just one example of internal opposition there, mirrored the relentless turning of the political tide against Concorde. It seemed to be increased rather than diminished by the steady success of the flight test programme. In March 1971 the Senate voted again not to spend any more money on Boeing's SST. President Nixon said then that he was 'distressed and disappointed' but was soon to lose interest as he became engulfed in the Watergate scandal. Commenting in the BBC news bulletins on the Senate decision I pointed out that it would strengthen the increasingly vocal opposition to Concorde in Britain and France:

'However . . . its long-term sales chances must be immensely improved if the British and French Governments don't now lose their nerve and decide to scrap it. Sales of over 200 up to 1980 aren't likely to be affected one way or the other, but after that Britain and France should have a virtual monopoly of supersonics in the Western world.'

BAC and Aerospatiale, defending the rising cost of Concorde, were to point out again and again that the US had spent more than $1 billion on their scrapped project with no return, and Boeing and General Electric, which was to provide

A technician making an internal introscope examination of one of 01's Rolls Royce/Snecma 593-4 engines — an important maintenance feature. *Rolls Royce*

the engines, had to lay off a total of 13,000 workers; against that a completed Concorde cost little more.

By the time 01 — the first 'pre-production' Concorde, nine feet longer than the prototypes — was rolled out at Filton at the end of March, there were 50,000 workers in Britain and France, divided among the aircraft and engine companies and their sub-contractor component makers, dependent upon the project. They grew increasingly anxious as the British and French ministers repeatedly postponed the decision to give the go-ahead and the funds to start full production work. It came at last in April, after a 5hr meeting of Anglo-French ministers — permission for each country to build two more Concordes, plus the release of £30 millions to place advance orders for materials for Concordes 11 to 16. But the ministers were cool and cautious and their communiqué omitted any expression of confidence in Concorde's future.

For air correspondents like myself the next step was to get a flight in Concorde — preferably before one's TV and newspaper rivals. It seemed a good idea to play BAC and Aerospatiale against one another, and BAC public relations men became satisfyingly alarmed when it seemed that one or two British correspondents might get a ride first in the French Concorde. Our hopes rose when the French President, M. Pompidou, took a 100min flight in 001 from Paris to Toulouse, including a spell at Mach 2 over the Bay of Biscay. Prime Minister Heath, although he had accepted an invitation to fly in 002 at some future date, spent that day sailing, as we were not slow to point out. But BAC did manage to get into what the French turned into a grand ceremonial occasion: they sought and obtained permission from the French for Brian Trubshaw to fly 002 to Toulouse so that when the President landed in 001 there could be joint congratulations. There were two newsmen aboard at last — my favourite cameraman, Bill Baglin of the BBC, filming on a pool basis for all interested TV networks, plus a Reuters man to write the words. I was at Toulouse to greet Bill enviously as he bounced off 001 full of enthusiasm and as usual with lots of excellent film.

Little use was made of the Reuters man's report: the newspapers wanted their own first-hand descriptions of a supersonic flight, and so of course did I. The Paris Air Show at the end of May was regarded by the air correspondents as their opportunity to fly in Concorde — and those prospects seemed to be much improved when the Russians flew in their Concordski, the Tu-144, two days before the Show opened, thus sharpening up the competition.

'Russia's supersonic airliner seemed no noisier than subsonic jets,' I reported. 'It looks even beakier than Concorde, for the droop-snoot is more sharply pointed. Carrying slightly fewer passengers, she's 200 miles faster, with a cruising speed of 1,500mph...On this prototype the pilots have ejection seats — not provided for Brian Trubshaw and Andre Turcat in the West. Far from having to use them, the Russians say their development programme, which has kept six months ahead of Concorde, is going well. Proving flights across Siberia should start this autumn, and they're looking for export orders at the Paris Air Show.'

The journalistic clamour for flights quickly sparked off a first-class Anglo-French row. The British air correspondents learned, to their chagrin, that ten French and one American journalist were to get a flight in 001, but that Henri Ziegler, head of Aerospatiale, had told BAC that there was no room for any

British correspondents. Eleven was the maximum possible number of passengers, because the the prototypes were still full of test equipment.

BAC told us, unconvincingly, that they had protested that this breached an unwritten agreement that the two countries should be equally represented on demonstration flights. Ziegler retorted that the British should have used their own Concorde — now back at Filton — to give us a flight; the French, he said, had done a great presentational job by carrying President Pompidou, who had become the first Head of State ever to fly in an uncertificated aircraft, and the British had failed to make similar efforts to create international confidence in Concorde's future. That was it, it seemed. The BAC public relations people departed to their luxury château for the night leaving the British press seething.

I imagined the sniggers at my expense on BBC newsdesks next day and decided to take matters into my own hands. With my *Daily Mail* friend Angus Macpherson providing moral support beside me I rang the Aerospatiale chalet, and demanded to speak to Henri Ziegler. I started mildly by expressing our concern about the proposal to carry French journalists with no British representation, and he at once repeated the line that there had never been any restriction by him on the British 'using their own Concorde' for Press demonstration flights, which in his view should have taken place already.

'But we regard 001 as half British, just as 002 is half French, and thus we are entitled to a half share of any news facilities.'

'I am having a hell of a time, with terrible letters, and it is not possible.' (Later I learned that the French journalists included a woman magazine writer reputed to be the mistress of a senior French minister.)

'If the French journalists are to have a supersonic flight, there must be one for the British journalists too.'

'But we are committed to flying Senator Barry Goldwater (given Ambassadorial rank by President Nixon to come to Europe to evaluate Concorde) after the French journalists' flight, and there are no more engine hours available for a third flight.'

'In that case I am not asking, I am demanding, that half the French journalists must be replaced by British journalists on tomorrow's flight.'

'I tell you it is absolutely impossible, because I am already fully committed, and I do not want to be shot by those to whom I am already committed.'

As I continued to insist, Ziegler became more and more emotional, insisting on the tremendous 'promotional' feat he had achieved, and repeating his criticism of BAC. His English deteriorated, and he sounded as if he were in tears:

'You can fight each other with machine guns, and while you fight I will sit away. I am fed up. I have done my best — better than anybody. I spend most of the day being addressed, so I won't come to the Show any more!'

But he did. Early the following morning we learned that he had persuaded Turcat to take up a group of British journalists immediately after the French had been flown. And my troubles began all over again. Our flight was to be late afternoon, and while it would be easy for me to send my radio pieces, to transmit my TV report I would ideally need an expensive 'unilateral' circuit. The Foreign News Editor was summoned from the golf course to authorise it.

But when he learned that there would not be room for a cameraman aboard, this self-important gentleman, already indignant at having his game interrupted,

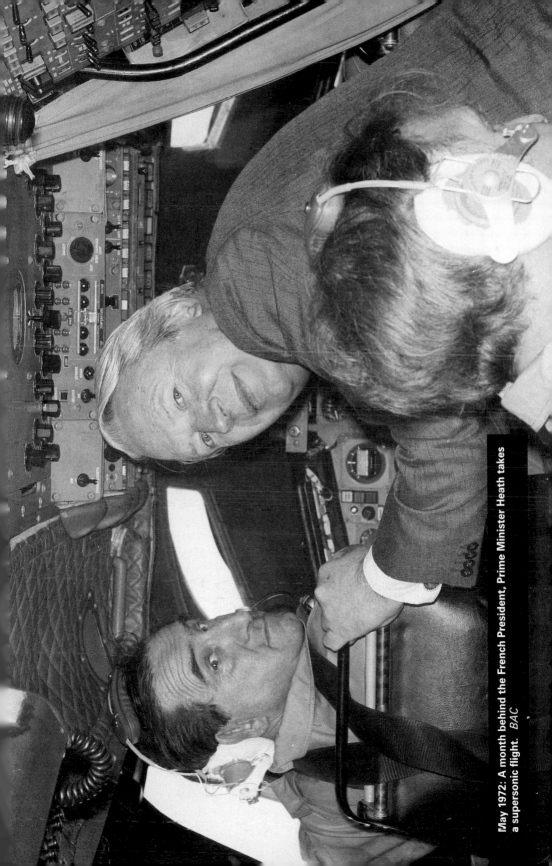

May 1972: A month behind the French President, Prime Minister Heath takes a supersonic flight. *BAC*

British Air Correspondents wait to board 001 for their first flight. Left to right: Frank Robson, *Daily Express*; A/Cdr Donaldson, *Daily Telegraph*; Michael Donne, *Financial Times* behind author; Angus Macpherson, *Daily Mail* and Mike Ramsden, *Flight International*.

retorted that 'he' was not paying for a unilateral just to put Turnill's face on the screen. I had no opportunity to point out that a cheaper alternative would be to illustrate my voiced report with Bill Baglin's film shot on his earlier flight. In any case I was otherwise occupied:

'Thirty minutes after take-off all 10 of us were crowded around Concorde's mach-meter, among flight-test consoles in what will later be the first-class passenger cabin. As it clicked up from 1.99 to Mach 2, we were 10 miles high over the Bay of Biscay. A landmark in anyone's career. But on the flight deck Andre Turcat's unflappable bald head didn't even turn.

'The take-off WAS noisy, for the prototype isn't fully soundproofed. But with 80 tons of thrust from the Rolls-Royce jets — including re-heat — we leapt into the sky like a dart in 29 seconds from a standing start. In ten minutes we were through the sound barrier, as we swept up past the Channel Islands. A few moments later, with the Scilly Isles below, a small thud and shudder. Turcat had turned on the fuel transfer system, which almost instantly switches five hundred gallons of fuel from the forward tanks to the tail — compensation for the fact that the aircraft's centre of gravity moves backward at supersonic speed. That was the one unusual sensation. Over the Bay of Biscay, now above Mach 2, doing 1,350 mph, we made the manoeuver which is really impressing the experts: a thirty degree U-turn. The stresses would break up any other air-craft in the world, with the exception probably of Russia's Tu-144. But on the flight deck the atmosphere was no different from that on a normal jetliner. Turcat was contentedly contemplating his instrument panel — all green, and no red lights. One instrument showed that if we were flying to New York, we'd get there in exactly 3hr from take-off at Paris. Another dial showed that the plane's wings and skin outside were hotter than boiling point — caused by friction as we rushed through the air. I put my hand on the window and inside it was quite cool.

'Our flight added 51 minutes to Concorde's total of well over 100 hours of supersonic flight. At the end, as we made two low runs over the Paris Air Show, we were astronauts, weightless as we turned sharply to come back — some-thing Concorde won't do in passenger service.

'Nearly two hours in Concorde has convinced me that huge crowded jumbo jets will quickly lose their appeal when supersonic flying starts. In this smaller plane one is still an individual; and the enormous speed restores the feeling that travelling can be an adventure rather than a dull routine.'

As my story — 'Duration 2'35" plus 25" cue; satisfactory quality' read the engineer's report — was going out on every BBC radio news programme that night I rang TV News' Editor-of-the-Day to ask what they proposed to do about it.

'Nothing!'

'Do you mean you are not even going to mention it?'

'That's correct.'

'I must advise you that you will be making a big mistake!'

I could hear him shrug as he put down the phone. Just over an hour later ITN's News at Ten led with Peter Sissons' story. Whether he realised that it had been entirely due to my efforts that he had got aboard I do not know — but it was a humiliating experience for me, to be deprived of the main fruits of my own efforts. Next morning every national newspaper also led with its own correspondent's story of what supersonic flight would be like. An 'inquest' followed on how BBC TV News came to miss the story, but I was too sick even to write them a complaining memo, and there was never a word of apology from them.

It was the ultimate example of why I never yielded to pressure to give up working for reliable old 'steam' radio in order to concentrate all my efforts on television.

Our flight also had an unhappy sequel for France's Concorde team. When the delayed flight for Senator Goldwater and ten airline chiefs took place, the afterburners failed to light when required to push 001's speed up to Mach 2. Jets had been clogged by a fuel additive used to reduce engine smoke during the Air Show demonstrations. Turcat had assigned his No.2, Gilbert Defer, to the pilot's seat for this flight, and he was bitterly disappointed. But Goldwater made light of it; they had flown supersonically, even if they had not passed the magic Mach 2; and, he added, 'If we don't wake up to the dreadful mistake we have made in cancelling our supersonic airliner, America will cease to be the world's leading technological country.'

Hurried departure of air correspondents to telephone descriptions of supersonic flight.

CHAPTER FIVE

How the Orders were Lost

When BOAC did get around to announcing a firm order for five Concordes at a cost of £65 millions, with another £50 millions to be spent on spare parts and hangars, the project suffered two more major blows to its sales prospects. Not only was the purchase price much higher than the French thought wise, but BOAC made the orders conditional upon obtaining supersonic 'corridors' over lightly populated areas — and the Government which had previously announced that no supersonic flying would be allowed over Britain, undertook to help the national airline to negotiate such corridors elsewhere. That was May 1972, and by then the first delivery had slipped to 'early 1975'.

However, BOAC was at last making positive, almost enthusiastic noises under its chairman Keith Granville, who denied that he had been 'pressured' by the Government into converting the airline's options into firm orders. Remarkably BOAC had announced its decision before Air France, in spite of Ziegler's 'promotions' and President Pompidou's flight. Concorde, Granville told me, would provide an all-first class service 'at a notch above' current first class fares. There would be supersonic routes to the United States, South Africa, Japan and Australia. Rashly, I added a forecast that the first supersonic corridor would be over Siberia to Tokyo, in return for reciprocal flying rights for the Soviets' Tu-144; but I was not to know that Concordski would turn out to be such a technical failure.

Ministerial confidence in the project had grown slowly, helped perhaps by the wives of John Davies, Trade and Industry Secretary, and Lord Carrington, Defence Secretary, who had been the first ministers to venture on a flight and sensibly took their wives with them. 'A fabulous aircraft which has now proved itself' Davies declared as he descended the steps to be confronted by my microphone — at last abandoning both his and the Government's careful neutrality. He believed that 150 could be built and sold by 1978 — at which point it could be called successful — but the sales target was in fact 250 by 1980.

Prince Philip added his reflected glory ('The extraordinary thing is that flying at twice the speed of sound is no different . . . all the genius is in the little boxes') by taking the controls during a 90min flight — though he had to cool his Royal heels for five hours because one of those red lights appeared just as Trubshaw was taxyng for the first attempted take-off.

Spurred by the French jibes, and encouraged by the fact that the pre-production 01 Concorde could take over the test-flight programmes, BAC won Government approval for 002 to undertake a global sales tour. February 1972 had marked the tenth anniversary of the Anglo-French agreement to embark on the project, and by now the 'options' or provisional orders by 16 airlines for 74 Concordes, once brandished as a reason why other airlines should join the queue before they fell too far behind, had become a major handicap.

Airlines like PanAm and TWA were holding grimly on to their options as an insurance, without having the least intention of converting them into firm orders until they had to. The option list, I pointed out in 'From Our Own Correspondent', which had in its time helped to avert cancellation, was now preventing the salesmen from getting the signed contracts which would force other airlines 'to form a neat and orderly supersonic queue'.

Japan was conscious that supersonic travel could at last end their long geographic isolation; but the national airline was tenth on the option list and under that its first delivery would be Concorde 39, due for completion in 1976. If the options queue could be broken, Japan could almost certainly be persuaded to sign a firm contract for much earlier deliveries. China, even though she still lacked a national airline, was eager to leap into the 20th century with Concorde orders — and so was Iran. Sir George Edwards, head of BAC, made a bid to win respectability for Concorde in the US — and with it conversion of options there into firm orders — by proposing that US planemakers, having had their SST project cancelled, should join Europe in collaborating on a second generation supersonic aircraft. Secor Browne, Chairman of the US Civil Aeronautics Board, welcomed the idea when I interviewed him — but firms like Boeing and Lockheed had little intention of agreeing; they thought themselves much too grand to play second fiddle to BAC and Aerospatiale. Harding Lawrence, chairman of Braniff International, which had given Edwards the launching order for the BAC One Eleven short-range jet, also wanted early deliveries — although he too needed supersonic corridors, in his case over the Panama isthmus. Lawrence encouraged the collaboration proposal with talk of 3,000mph hypersonic aircraft in passenger operation by 1990.

When the sales tour did take place, in June 1972, it was at that time the most elaborate and expensive sales tour ever undertaken by Britain. Because it would last a month, Brian Trubshaw took the view that 'something was bound to go wrong'.

So Concorde was accompanied by a RAF Belfast freighter carrying a spare engine and all the components that might possibly develop faults, as well as an RAF Super VC10 carrying about 70 technicians, officials and public relations men. So that it could carry news media to cover the tour, and give demonstration flights to as many VIPs as possible, 002's seating capacity had been increased to 16, even though it was still largely filled with 12 tons of test equipment which would be needed later for thousands of hours of high temperature and low altitude trials. The British Government was paying, and I estimated —

84

Left: **Prince Philip takes the right-hand seat to fly 002 from Fairford.** *de Coninck*

Below: **Prince Philip, flanked by Sir George Edwards and Brian Trubshaw, holds his postflight news conference.** *de Coninck*

002 providing an excellent view of engines and intakes as it comes in to land at Fairford. *BAC*

conservatively, I would guess now — that 'there would be little change out of £200,000'.

I was responsible for a small part of the cost, because I was provided with a ticket aboard a routine flight to Singapore, to join Concorde there and accompany it to Tokyo.

With his wife Anne, Michael Heseltine, newly appointed Minister for Aerospace under John Davies of the DTI, was aboard Concorde for the first part of the tour. Heseltine was a young man with a hairstyle which soon earned him the nickname 'Tarzan' and with ambitions which he did not hide, and even a timetable for when he aimed to become Prime Minister. In his first public speech in his new post, three weeks before the tour started, Heseltine had committed himself wholeheartedly to the project, pointing out that it meant 30,000 jobs in the UK when production peaked. Each Concorde, when sold abroad, would bring 'the best part of £15 millions in foreign exchange'; and BOAC Concordes, able to cross the Atlantic four times a day would earn £10,000 or more on each flight, at least half of which would be in foreign exchange. 'Quite clearly there can be no question of allowing regular sonic booms to take place over our cities or other densely populated areas. At the same time there seems to me no justification for banning sonic booms over uninhabited or virtually uninhabited deserts and other wastelands...It is impossible to resist a feeling of pride to be connected with this remarkable project.'

I was at Singapore in time to cover the arrival there, and to hear an enthusiastic Heseltine declaring that, on the route via Athens, Teheran, Bahrain, Bombay and Bangkok, they had cut flight times 'beyond our wildest dreams.' At Tehran 'His Imperial Majesty the Shah' had been allowed to occupy 002's left-hand (the commander's) seat throughout Mach 2 flight, and announced that he would start negotiations to purchase Concordes and would provide a supersonic corridor through Iran's sparsely inhabited areas.

Brian Trubshaw described what it was like landing for the first time at Bombay: 'The weather was quite nice, but I thought it was a very funny-looking airport,' he said. 'Then I realised that masses of people from the Air India maintenance base and elsewhere had broken through the barriers and were lining the sides of the runway. It was like landing on a football pitch, with people standing and sitting on both sides, waving at us as we came in'.

Before the tour began the Anti-Concorde Project had done its best to sour the whole thing by sending advance letters to the Governments and other bodies warning of the horrors that supersonic aircraft would bring, but so far without any effect at all. An enthusiastic crowd of 4,000 was at Singapore Airport to watch Brian Trubshaw circle twice before landing, so that he would touch down on time and not early. Lee Kuan Yew, Singapore's Prime Minister, was allowed to take his son and daughter, aged 14 and 16, on his demonstration flight — the first children to sample supersonics. Singapore too would buy Concordes, it was announced — 'if the makers could prove that they would make a profit'.

Heseltine and his entourage went reluctantly back to London and the political scrum, and were replaced on the tour by Lord Jellicoe, the Lord Privy Seal, and Lady Jellicoe. There was now room aboard Concorde for Frank Robson of the Daily Express and myself. We had an extra day in Singapore, because, as Trubshaw forecast, something did go wrong. The technicians aboard the VC10 justified their journey by sorting out a recurrence of trouble with the afterburners and a problem with the weather radar, and we departed for what should have been a restful overnight stop at Manila.

In fact everyone — including, to my alarm, Brian Trubshaw on whose skill our safety depended — was kept up all almost all night by international bickering involving ambassadors, civil servants, airport chiefs, air traffic controllers and the Concorde sales team. In the way of Britain's civil servants, our Manila representatives had not bothered to mention that the lost day meant that we were arriving on the eve of the Philippines' Independence Day; they assumed everybody would know that. But as soon as we did arrive Government officials and the local air traffic controllers said that Concorde must leave before 7am next morning, because the capital's airport would be closed for military air displays. They were determined not to have their Independence Day flypasts upstaged by a Concorde take-off in the middle of it all. That would mean however that if Concorde was to arrive at Tokyo's Haneda Airport at the agreed local time of 11am, we would have to remain airborne for an hour longer than our prototype's limited fuel capacity would permit.

In Tokyo, however, where the Philippine celebrations seemed of little significance, and where the advance communications from the Anti-Concorde Project had made a much greater impact, it was suspected that BAC's request for an earlier arrival time was a wicked Concordian plot. Already Concorde had dodged some elaborate anti-Concorde demonstrations planned for the original Sunday arrival by being a day late; now arrival an hour early would mean that the eager environmentalists would not be back in position in time to condemn our black smoke and measure our noise levels with their rather ancient 'phon' machines. Quite how it was resolved I never managed to discover; I do remember that after two uneasy hours in bed, we were all up again at 4am local time to be bussed back to the airport.

At Haneda Airport it was a sultry, overcast day — the worst possible conditions for Concorde, which I reported, 'arrived amid a cloud of its own black smoke', thus fulfilling all the worst forecasts.

Soon Lord Jellicoe had his back to the wall facing hostile Japanese journalists — very different from the respectful representatives of the firmly controlled Press at the earlier stops. The British Government, Jellicoe assured them, were just as worried about cleaning up the environment as the Japanese; and everybody would see for themselves that smoke was eliminated and noise decreased when the fourth Concorde, with improved Rolls Royce engines, made its first flight from Toulouse in three months' time. Then why had he not waited and brought that to Tokyo, they demanded?

The President of Japan Air Lines said there were five problems to be solved before they would consider converting their three options into firm orders: reliability, fatigue, range, economics and noise.

The sales team had been expecting tough negotiations from the Japanese, but they were taken aback by the hostility of the Press coverage — enormous headlines meaning 'The Black Smoke was Awful' and 'The Monstrous Bird'. The latter was doubly wounding, because it was the lead in the six-million circulation *Mainichi Shimbun*, which had arranged to promote Concorde as part of its centenary celebrations. I also described how, on eight TV channels, presenters of 30min programmes repeated with relish the long-since disproved charges that supersonic flights would pollute the upper atmosphere, and summoned

Left: **Relief at the end of Prince Philip's delayed 90min flight over the Bay of Biscay. He is flanked by John Cochrane, left, and Brian Trubshaw. Sir George Edwards is last but one on the steps.** *de Coninck*

Below: **May 1972: BOAC's Chairman, Keith Granville, at last signs the airline's order for five Concordes. With spares, etc, it totalled £115 millions.** *de Coninck*

Government officials (who were apparently obliged to respond) to ask: 'After all that are you still thinking of buying Concorde?'

There was a hint of what was to follow, though few then took it seriously, when the BBC Foreign Desk in London rang asking me to follow up an Associated Press report that Pan American Airways had told other airlines that for economic reasons it had decided not to exercise its options to buy eight Concordes. PanAm was a key player in the game, for it was the only foreign airline entitled to delivery of Concordes at the same time as BOAC and Air France. Derek John, BAC's Concorde Marketing Director, gave me a quote saying that no official message had been received from PanAm, and I sent a piece from Tokyo pointing out that this airline had been 'deep in the red' for two years. Unable to afford to take up its own options, PanAm, which used to be the trend-setter in ordering new aircraft, was now trying to persuade its rivals at least to delay their entry into the supersonic race.

Concorde 002 flew on to more controversy in Australia, while I flew back to London to cover such things as the BEA Trident disaster. But with Michael Heseltine I went to Toulouse to be on board the final leg of 002's 40,000 miles tour as it returned to Heathrow flying the British and French flags and claiming that it had all been a great triumph. Brian Trubshaw had certainly proved that Concorde was technically operational, and told me: 'You can't embark on a project like this and not have some against you and I think that many people were very surprised that the boom is much less innocuous than they imagined.' For the only time in its career, Concorde had in fact been allowed to fly supersonically over five different countries, including two supersonic stages of 2,000 miles between Darwin and Sydney and Melbourne back to Darwin. 'There were hardly any published reports of disturbance' claimed BAC, supplementing Lord Jellicoe's claim that Concordes had flown above 10,000 ships without complaint.

Bad news and good news followed within days. First Air Canada announced that it had cancelled its four Concorde options saying that 'at the moment' it was not suitable for their services.

I played this down after consulting BAC and Government sources, pointing out that early Concordes would not in fact have sufficient range for Europe-Canada routes, and that the cancellations might actually be helpful in freeing options for customers like Iran whose national airline wanted three.

The good news was that China then ordered three Concordes, — two from France and one from Britain — becoming the first customer actually to sign a contract with Aerospatiale for two, since BOAC and Air France were still negotiating the details of the orders they had announced.

Before 1972 was out I was back at Toulouse yet again — with 1500 VIPs and newsmen flown there from all over the world for a double roll-out. The star this time was the first European Airbus, built by a five-nation consortium which the British Government had refused to join, ceremonially rolled out with the French-built 'pre-production' Concorde 02, with the more advanced Rolls- Royce engines, and which the French had dubbed the *ne fume pas Concorde*.

That was the day when it became clear to me that much Concorde money was being used to establish Toulouse as the centre of European aviation.

There was always a strong element of wishful thinking about French programmes, and sometimes it was so determined and concentrated that the wishes came true. Wishful thinking was undoubtedly behind a piece that

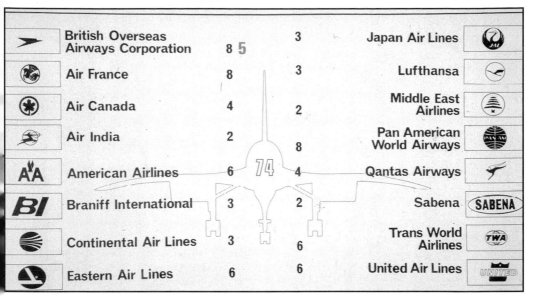

➤	British Overseas Airways Corporation	8 5	3	Japan Air Lines		JAL
🐎	Air France	8	3	Lufthansa		⌒
✳	Air Canada	4	2	Middle East Airlines		▲
⤴	Air India	2	8	Pan American World Airways		PAN AM
AA	American Airlines	6	4	Qantas Airways		✈
BI	Braniff International	3	2	Sabena	SABENA	
≋	Continental Air Lines	3	6	Trans World Airlines	TWA	
◤	Eastern Air Lines	6	6	United Air Lines	UNITED	

Above: **BAC's list of airlines holding Concorde options.**

Below: **Gen Ziegler of Aerospatiale making a presentation to a Japanese delegation when it was hoped that they would buy Concorde.** *Aerospatiale*

appeared in November in the French daily news sheet, *Aerospace,* reporting that PanAm had decided to buy five Concordes.

It came as an anodyne just after United became the first of the seven US airlines which had held options for nearly 10 years to cancel them.

This was then explained away on the ground that United Airlines had no long overseas routes suitable for supersonic operations. I described the news that PanAm would buy as 'premature' — but it influenced me, and even more BAC and Aerospatiale, into believing that there was hope yet that PanAm would lead the world's airlines into the supersonic age despite its four years of heavy operating losses and excessive investment in 35 of the new Boeing 747 jumbo jets.

But for PanAm a clock had started ticking when BOAC and Air France had finally signed their contracts with BAC in London and Aerospatiale in Paris to buy respectively five and four aircraft.

In return for agreeing either to cancel their options or convert them into firm contracts within six months of the BOAC/Air France contracts, PanAm had cleverly obtained the right to buy every third Concorde produced up to No 18. Thus, they had the right to match any Concorde services from London and Paris with equal services of their own — or, if they now cancelled their options, to influence the other US option holders to cancel theirs. For Concorde's salesmen therefore 31 January 1973 had become make-or-break day.

For once I covered it all from London. Geoffrey Knight, BAC's chief Concorde salesman — he was also deputy chairman — moved his office to a comfortable New York hotel soon after Christmas, and spent most of the month vainly striving to forestall the ultimate disaster. Occasionally he rang Weybridge in Surrey to instruct one of his expert presenters to catch the next plane as he made the round of Pan American's bankers to explain to them that, despite their financial problems, US airlines *must* order Concordes; if they did not, BOAC and Air France would cream off all the first-class passengers, and the financial plight of the US airlines would be even worse. A reception was given at BAC's hotel for about 100 bankers who had come from all over the US to hear Concorde presentations. Michael Heseltine attended the reception, the atmosphere was friendly and spirits rose. But against that, Knight had increasing difficulty in gaining admittance to the PanAm headquarters a few blocks from his hotel. As he himself records, he began to feel that no contracts would be forthcoming by the end of January, and what he must fight for was to avoid cancellation of the options by offering PanAm an extension of the deadline.

My TV and radio progress reports jumped into the lead on Sunday, 20 January, when *The Observer* newspaper, whose air correspondent, Andrew Wilson, had conducted an implacable anti-Concorde campaign, carried a front page headline, datelined New York: 'US Airlines Turn Down Concorde'. Although it seems that no final decision had been taken by the full PanAm board, Wilson had clearly had more success than Geoffrey Knight in gaining access to the executives who mattered. That day Sir George Edwards, BAC's chairman, whom I described as the 'Father figure of British aviation' also flew to New York to add his final pleas to the US airline chiefs he knew so well not to cancel the options.

On the 31st, on radio and TV, I was counting down the hours as the deadline for the PanAm decision ran out. It came just in time for me to change the tenses in my final TV report at 11.15 pm.

Above: **Michael Heseltine, Minister for Aerospace,** at the beginning of his political career, seen here after a Concorde flight with Princess Margaret, agreed to BOAC's demand for an operating subsidy. *de Coninck*

Left: **Jack de Coninck, BAC film director,** who took many photos included here, beside the passenger cabin machmeter. Nowadays Concorde's speed is kept down to Mach 2.00 to reduce wear on the airframe. *de Coninck*

1973: Concorde production peaks: Five front fuselage sections on the Filton production line. *BAC*

Geoffrey Knight had been presented with this humiliating Press statement: 'Pan American will not exercise its options to purchase Concorde. PanAm's studies indicate that the airplane will be capable of scheduled supersonic service, but since it has significantly less range, less payload and higher operating costs than are provided by the current and prospective wide-bodied jets, it will require substantially higher fares than today's. Concorde does not appear to be an airliner that satisfies PanAm's future objectives and future requirements as the company now sees them.'

With some difficulty Knight got another sentence added before the Press statement was issued: 'However, PanAm will maintain an "open door" to the manufacturers of Concorde for any new proposal they may wish to make.'

As expected, TWA also cancelled their options within hours of the announcement, and I began describing the Tu-144 as 'Concorde's best friend,' and speculating that instead of starting on the North Atlantic, the supersonic age would start with competing Concorde and Tu-144 services operating over Siberia to Japan. But next day the president of Japan Air Lines poured cold water over that prospect by describing the PanAm and TWA decisions as 'a good guideline on policy,' and said there was little prospect that they would extend their options.

Despite the fact that there were by then four Concorde prototypes flying, and the first four passenger aircraft were in an advanced state of assembly, the future of the project once again looked bleak. Late next day Sir George Edwards agreed to give a news conference, and for once both radio and TV provided their Outside Broadcast vehicles for the use of a News Division correspondent. They blocked the road outside the central London office where it took place; and with the 6pm Radio News almost due, both ITN and the newspaper correspondents agreed that I should have first crack at the great man. My fellow air correspondents had long since accepted that direct questions from me in front of TV cameras, with the interviewee conscious that millions would watch and judge him for frankness and honesty as he answered, were likely to extract more direct replies than the usual verbal fencing at a news conference.

Coverage of the whole drama was massive, and after seeing and hearing the overnight and morning news bulletins, Charles Gardner declared a truce in our normal hostilities and sent me a letter, no doubt at the prompting of George Edwards, who had by then learned how counter-productive it was to write such things to the BBC Chairman or Director General:

'Dear Reg — If I may say so without sounding stuffy, your BBC coverage of the Concorde crisis was absolutely first-rate — factual, objective and fair and everyone here has commented on it. Thanks a great deal — on behalf of (as they say) BAC and especially on behalf of me and my chaps. I was glad to be able to do a bit back — by preserving your "exclusive" position at the Press Conference.' The last sentence was a bit puzzling, but was apparently a reference to the fact that, by general agreement, I interviewed Edwards first — with everyone else gathered around out of shot — for the early radio and TV bulletins. Such letters of course were calculated to soften one up; but I resisted the temptation when describing the occasion in what I felt was one of my best contributions a few days later to 'From Our Own Correspondant':

'For me the most moving and unexpected moment of this week's chapter in the Concorde saga came when Sir George Edwards, head of the British Aircraft

Corporation, faced the Press. The occasion had a rarity value in itself, for it's something he seldom does nowadays.

'Though he once described himself to me as "indestructible", he is at present a physically frail man, recovering from two major operations in the last year or two. One wondered whether that had induced a rare twinge of conscience in the collective mind of Authority, with the result that last year he was awarded Britain's highest and most coveted honour — the Order of Merit. The only honour, incidentally, that Bernard Shaw would have accepted.

'Now that Russia's Tupolev is dead, Sir George, though he's only 64, is the last survivor of the individualistic, creative aviation pioneers — with the possible exception of France's Marcel Dassault. There just won't be any more Wright and Short Brothers, Handley Pages and Sydney Camms. Nowadays, creation can only be achieved by groups of young mathematicians crouched over computers.

'All the same, when Sir George began by saying it had been a tiring two weeks, and he'd forgotten his glasses, and could he talk sitting down, it was clear he was feeling a little sorry for himself. I don't think I was alone in feeling momentarily out of sympathy with him. One sensed that the collective air correspondent reaction was that feeling tired wasn't going to solve the problems of Concorde, and of all the men and jobs now involved in it throughout Britain and France.

'So the questions took on a somewhat sharp note, and quickly elicited the fact that he felt the Concorde project must be "rolled down" as he put it — even if it involved the painful choice of closing down either the production line at Filton, or its twin at Toulouse. That brought out the leadership qualities. We were quickly and justly rebuked for our jingoism. Suddenly he was looking into the 21st century. He's always seen Concorde as a 30-year project, he said. What mattered was not whether, in the short term, we had to give up our production lines in favour of the French — or they theirs in favour of Filton. All that mattered was the long-term survival of the Concorde project...

'Though it's a bit late now, the basic question is still whether Concorde was the right thing to do in the first place. But the fact is (and no one inside aviation really disputes it) that supersonics *was* the inevitable next step: just as, in space, once it had become possible to place men in earth orbit, the next logical step was to send them to the moon.

'"But it's too noisy, too dirty and too expensive — and anyway no one wants it", is the burden of the environmental opposition.

'It would be easier to sympathise with the demands for less noise and more cleanliness if the environmental organisations were equally vocal about cleaning up the plastic filth that litters our cities, and the sewage in our seas. It's fallen to me to cover very closely both space and supersonics. Somehow man's destiny is taking him into these fields quite irresistibly; who can really deny that there is a tide in the affairs of men?

'Clearly it's reasonable to insist that even if we do have to go with the supersonic tide, we must make sure that we don't swamp our population with noise and pollute our atmosphere with water vapour. But, trying to stand back and view in perspective the battles of our modern St George, and the enthusiastic seven-day weeks worked voluntarily throughout both the space and aviation industries, is it too far-fetched to suspect that some of the aggressive and even violent opposition evoked by their grand projects stems from a deep and primeval resentment of the fact that these men actually enjoy their work?'

96

Concorde intakes — exterior and interior views.   *de Coninck*

Sir George, I was quickly informed by Charles Gardner, was very upset by this piece; but I wrote him a brief conciliatory note, and his reply implied that I was forgiven — borne out by friendly meetings and ready interviews in later years.

In a nice display of defiance, France's Concorde 02 made non-stop flights of over 6,000km from Toulouse first to Iceland and back, and then to West Africa and back, mostly at Mach 2, demonstrating its ability to fly the Paris-New York and Frankfurt-New York routes. All the same, between those flights the whole option system was abandoned and all deposits were returned to the airlines.

While that was happening I was accompanying Mrs Bhutto, wife of the then President of Pakistan, on a formal visit to China. The only other journalists invited were the two who had become famous for their anti-Concorde writings — Andrew Wilson of *The Observer*, who it was impossible to deny had had a world scoop by getting the PanAm decision long before anyone else; and Mary Goldring of *The Economist,* a favourite interviewee of BBC radio and TV current affairs programmes, which revelled in her predictions that no more than nine passenger Concordes would ever be built. I got the impression that they expected to be summoned by Prime Minister Chou En-lai to explain to him why he should cancel China's Concorde orders. No such summons ever came, but during a banquet in the Great Hall of the People, one of them did manage to ask him about the expansion plans for China's civil airline.

We had in fact seen how subsonic jets bought from Russia and Britain over a period of years were still parked at Peking Airport, rarely used, so it was not surprising, though disappointing for Wilson and Goldring, that Chou En-lai merely replied that it was 'a very difficult question to answer'.

Nine technicians working in cramped conditions on a flight deck assembly.
de Coninck

CHAPTER SIX

'Le Jour de Gloire'

Fears that cancellation of the US options would mean at last cancellation of the whole Concorde project were once again not fulfilled. On the contrary, indignation aroused by American rejection of Europe's enterprise had a dramatic unifying effect.

The Government and the Opposition spoke with one voice, with statements of confidence in Concorde from Michael Heseltine and Wedgwood Benn, now more comfortable as Opposition spokesman on Aerospace. The trade unions added their support. As for the national airlines, BOAC, briefly putting aside its domestic campaign for subsidies to operate the plane, described Concorde as 'a damned fine airplane', while the head of Air France pointed out that after 1975 there would be two kinds of airlines — 'those with Concorde and those without'.

For me there was then a welcome break from Concorde stories for some months, because for much of 1973 I was occupied with the Skylab space missions. I was in Houston, covering the rather desperate attempts by Pete Conrad and his crew to repair their damaged space laboratory, and missing the Paris Air Show for the first time since becoming Air Correspondent, when on Sunday afternoon, 3 June, the radio newsdesk rang to say that Concordksi, the Tu-144, had crashed. After having news agency descriptions read over to me, I reported in the 6pm News:

'First reports suggest that, as happens all too often at air shows, the crash may have resulted from an over-enthusiastic demonstration by the pilot, rather than any fault of the Tu-144 itself. But in any case, a setback like this for the Soviet supersonic plane is a setback for Concorde too; it's the competition provided by the Russians that's likely to persuade customers like Japan to go ahead with quick Concorde orders rather than wait for another two years or so. Since we saw Russia's supersonic plane at the last Paris Air Show, it's been completely redesigned. In fact, an American assessment of this much improved production plane was that its only resemblance to the original prototype was the Aeroflot paint!'

My quick assessment of the crash from 4,000 miles away was based partly on the few facts that were available, but much more on having witnessed all too many air show crashes. The French Concorde test pilot, Jean Franchi, had earlier given a very advanced and graceful demonstration, including touch-and-go landings on the runway, and very tight turns in between, to an ecstatic French

Above: **Paris Air Show 1973: The Tu-144 demonstrating just before it crashed.**
J. M. Ramsden

Right: **Jean Franchi, then Aerospatiale's Concorde chief test pilot, gave the 1973 Paris Air Show demonstration which the Tu-144 was trying to match just before it crashed.** *Aerospatiale*

crowd of 300,000. I had no doubt that the Soviet pilot felt he had to match, and preferably surpass, that performance with the Tu-144. His aircraft got into a steep dive, an overstressed wing snapped off, and first reports said he had he plunged into a nearby village, killing eight residents as well as the crew of five — figures that were to change later.

My friend Robert Hotz, Editor of *Aviation Week*, who had made the colourful assessment of the redesigned Concordski which crashed, gave me the material for another piece on Soviet supersonics three weeks later. The anti-supersonics lobby had failed to make much impression with their efforts to generate sinister propaganda out of the crash, but all the same the Soviets, still harbouring their own sales hopes, had allowed three US aviation writers into the secret factory near Moscow engaged on Tu-144 production.

Hotz took a photograph of five nearly-completed Tu-144s rolling along the production line, in addition to the five already built. At that stage Aeroflot was planning to operate a fleet of between 60 and 75 supersonic aircraft, and within a year the Moscow factory expected to be completing one every three weeks. 'As for the sonic boom, the Russians say that problem has been much exaggerated: they intend to operate their own huge fleet supersonically over their own territory all the time — probably starting just before Concorde's first passenger flight in two years' time', I reported.

The report of the Franco-Soviet accident investigation team into the Tu-144 crash was never published; it was a year later, again with help from Hotz, and the American astronauts and engineers who by then were regular visitors to Russia, that I was able to report that the combination of events which led to the crash was far more dramatic than any of us could have envisaged:

'For the investigators, the story began with the discovery of four bodies, instead of three, in the wreckage of the flight deck, with a damaged cine camera. From there they worked backwards. It was known that one of the three Soviet engineers on board had promised to do some filming for French TV. It was probably because he hadn't finished that the pilot, Captain Kozlov, flew on instead of landing as instructed. Then he caught sight of a French Air Force Mirage-3, also filming. Thinking he was on a collision course, Kozlov pushed the nose of the Tu-144 down to pass underneath the fighter — and the Soviet engineer, not strapped in as he was filming, was thrown on to the controls. That put the plane into a steep dive. Desperately he was dragged off, and emergency action taken to get the plane out of its dive. But Kozlov had to pull it up so steeply that the airframe was overstressed. First a wing broke off, then the tail, then the droop-snoot nose. As well as the crew of six, nine people were killed as it crashed on a small town six miles from the Air Show.'

In the meantime BAC and Aerospatiale at last got their chance to demonstrate the Anglo-French Concorde in the US. Dallas and Fort Worth had overcome their traditional rivalry sufficiently to agree to build and share a huge new international airport in the open countryside between their two cities. Already it had cost £300 millions and that was planned to increase to more than £1,000 millions by the year 2000.

Although it was far from ready for passenger services, the then Governor of Texas, John Connally, was determined that its opening should make world news. Britain and France were accordingly invited to send a Concorde, representative of the supersonic 21st century, to make an inaugural flypast and landing.

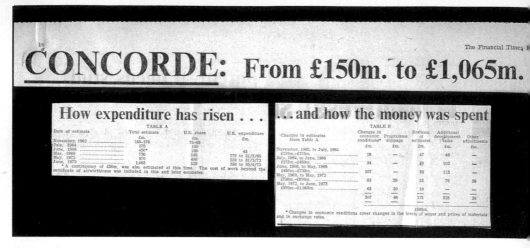

Above: **Costs pass £1 billion.**

Below: **The *Guardian* reacts.**

After worrying a great deal about possible anti-noise demonstrations the two Governments, BAC and Aerospatiale agreed that France should send 02, the 'ne fume pas'. Concorde, on a sales tour to Venezuela, Fort Worth, and back via Washington's Dulles Airport for the first US-Europe record-breaking flight.

The few residents in the vast area taken over by the new airport — 'a super air harbour' the Texans dubbed it — were more interested in the expected 40,000 jobs to be created than in anti-noise demonstrations. And the Texans made sure that the Ambassadors representing 50 nations, and the 8,000 guests invited ('bring a black tie for the Charity Ball!') with 12 bands to entertain them, would be enthusiasts, not troublemakers. I was sent a first-class air ticket to attend, but only after phone calls had been made to check my credentials. Mary Goldring and Andrew Wilson I would guess were not invited!

Because Fort-Worth/Dallas Airport was to be the headquarters of Braniff Airlines, a great effort was made to use the occasion to wring a firm Concorde order out of them. So Concorde 02 had been painted in British Airways livery, on one side (BOAC and BEA having recently been merged), and in Air France livery on the other.

Opportunistically, David Nicolson, the recently-appointed part time chairman of British Airways, flew in subsonically with journalists eager to watch and film Concorde's arrival, and filled in the waiting time by holding a news conference on how he planned to operate his Concorde fleet. By catching the 9am flight from London, he said, business men could overtake the clock to arrive in New York before 8am. After a five hour conference they could catch the afternoon Concorde back to London, and be in bed by 10.30pm. More than 90% of current first-class passengers, he claimed, were prepared to pay an extra 10% for the service.

Captain Jimmy Andrews, British Airways' Concorde flight manager, shared the sighs of relief as 02 arrived on time, emitting only the merest wisp of smoke and made a low flypast so that the French could film its Air France livery. Then it was supposed to make a similar flypast in the opposite direction, so that the British could film the British Airways' livery. But to our great indignation Jean Franchi, the pilot, suddenly opened the throttles and zoomed up to 3,000ft. Later we learned that the Control Tower had spotted a small Cessna, which was loaded with photographers in the centre of Franchi's flight path and only three miles ahead. 'Can you get out fast?' the Controller called to Franchi. 'I sure can,' he replied — and we had to wait for the landing before getting our national views of 02.

The whole occasion was a great success. Concorde took up coveys of Ambassadors and airline chiefs, and the tuxedoed guests at the charity ball queued in their hundreds to walk through the aircraft parked nearby. The stars of the flying display next day were a Vulcan bomber powered by early versions of the Concorde engines, which had first appeared at Farnborough 20 years earlier, vertical take-off Harriers, and finally Concorde itself. Awards were made to General Ziegler, Sir George Edwards, Andre Turcat and Brian Trubshaw — in the case of the last two, the Harmon Trophy for Aviation, awarded by President Nixon, a supersonic enthusiast, after 02 had made a subsonic flight to Dulles Airport. As I had forecast to dubious BAC officials the approach roads were blocked when Concorde arrived at Washington — not with protesters, but with aviation enthusiasts eager to see the aircraft. There were reassurances from various official bodies that Concorde would in due course get its US Certificate of Airworthiness. And from Dulles the first supersonic North Atlantic crossing was triumphantly completed in 213min.

There was still no order from Braniff Airlines, but George Edwards disclosed that the Anglo-French sales team were (rather desperately, I thought) proposing deals under which British Airways would lease Concordes for use by Braniff and Viasa, the Venezuelan airline, as well as to Australia's Qantas. The aim was to ensure that none of the 16 passenger Concordes due to be completed by the end of 1974 would remain parked and idle.

The warmth of the welcome for Concorde in the US, the fact that it passed its noise tests, and the complete failure of the British-led Anti-Concorde Project's campaign to spread its protest movement abroad, provided a welcome respite — during which Concorde's builders started some valuable work in conjunction with the National Aeronautics and Space Administration. America's National Academy of Sciences, investigating reports that supersonic aircraft flying above 60,000ft could damage the ozone layer, had concluded that a fleet of 800 supersonic aircraft, with 200 of them always flying, would cause no serious atmospheric effects. Now, by arrangement with the British Government, NASA provided some highly-sensitive infra-red devices to measure the exact composition of the atmosphere up to 80,000ft, and these were fitted to 02 for a series of flights over the Bay of Biscay and the Arctic Circle. Michael Heseltine announced that development costs had topped £1,000 millions — a story so often predicted that it attracted little notice when it came — and BAC and Aerospatiale campaigned quietly for more money to re-shape the wingtips to reduce fuel consumption. But then came the great oil crisis and the gradual build up of yet another 'Cancel Concorde' campaign. The Arab countries had finally got together to restrict oil production and raise prices, and Christmas 1973 brought fuel rationing for the airlines. The five Concordes by then in the flight-test programme would, however, get enough to continue the programme throughout 1974, said the Minister.

But the steep rise in operating costs resulting from the oil crisis was the final blow to sales prospects. British Airways' chairman announced that they would have to charge 30% above normal first-class fares to make Concorde pay, and Lufthansa said that that made the aircraft impossible for them. Industrial disputes in Britain had slowed down production, to the fury of the French, who were held up for lack of components. I went to Fairford to watch Brian Trubshaw bring in the sixth Concorde, No 202, at the end of February, four months late. He parked it alongside 002, just about to be retired; and when he strolled across to me to do the standard TV interview he echoed my own thoughts with his first comment: 'What a pity it isn't already in service.'

With no more orders, reducing production and laying off workers was by then the subject of regular Anglo-French meetings. The French had been arguing strongly that it should continue at the rate of eight per year. But suddenly Henri Ziegler who had fought so long and hard for the project, was removed as head of Aerospatiale, and French enthusiasm cooled. They argued that production should be cut to four a year, as if it had been their own idea — even though that was just what the British had been advocating.

And then the six-year-old Heath Government fell, and Wilson's Labour regime was in power again. Soon Wedgwood Benn, back as Secretary for

Production version of the Olympus engine claimed to be 'virtually smoke-free at all power settings, including after-burning'. New features in the production versions included higher mass flow low pressure compressor, an annular combustor with vaporising burners and the new Type 28 exhaust system. *Rolls-Royce*

Right: **Montage of newspaper headlines.**
Graham Turnill

As the enemies of the superjet mass for the kill,
one man is given the power to decide its future

This could be the kiss of death for Concorde

DAVID NICHOLSON, the outgoing British Airways chairman, ... admit to a

William Lowther

NGER . . . IN
SUDDENLY
ENT WORLD

THREAT

Let's try Concorde before we buy it — Pan Am president

BY MICHAEL DONNE, AEROSPACE CORRESPONDENT

A suggestion that a small group of the world... allowed to fly the Anglo-French Concor... service before it goes into quasi-... Najeeb Halaby, presiden...

Concorde costs escalate by £95m but Britain and France go ahead

By Arthur Reed
Air Correspondent

Below: **Press release from Anti-Concorde Project.**
Graham Turnill

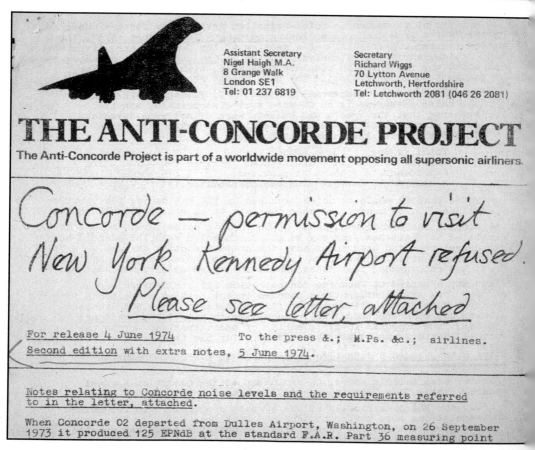

Assistant Secretary
Nigel Haigh M.A.
8 Grange Walk
London SE1
Tel: 01 237 6819

Secretary
Richard Wiggs
70 Lytton Avenue
Letchworth, Hertfordshire
Tel: Letchworth 2081 (046 26 2081)

THE ANTI-CONCORDE PROJECT

The Anti-Concorde Project is part of a worldwide movement opposing all supersonic airliners.

Concorde — permission to visit New York Kennedy Airport refused. Please see letter, attached

For release 4 June 1974   To the press &.; M.Ps. &c.; airlines.
Second edition with extra notes, 5 June 1974.

Notes relating to Concorde noise levels and the requirements referred
to in the letter, attached.

When Concorde 02 departed from Dulles Airport, Washington, on 26 September
1973 it produced 125 EPNdB at the standard F.A.R. Part 36 measuring point

Industry, was holding a news conference to publish the full financial details of the project. 'Tonight, it's hard to see how Concorde can survive,' was the way I started my TV News report. 'Mr Benn said Concorde's future had no pluses.

'Even if we break through and sell a hundred, we shall still lose more money. There were five options: cancel now, and pay out £80 millions for compensation and redundancy payments for 21,000 workers; complete the 16 under construction, which would mean losses of £205 millions on top of the £485 million already spent by Britain; complete 19, as the French proposed, with minor improvements, involving an extra loss of £220 millions; cut production to four a year, with major improvements — an extra loss of £390 millions; or finally, continue full production plus major modifications, resulting in a slight dip to losses of £385 millions.'

Labour Governments traditionally produced lots of alarming figures on the pretext that they were at last revealing to the public what had for long been hidden from them, and the only safe course was to report what they said in the knowledge that Governments always massaged figures to justify what they intended to do. And British Airways were quick to help by announcing that as a result of the energy crisis the £6 millions a year profit they hoped to get from their five Concordes could turn into a £26 millions a year loss. 'We see nothing that incites *us* to pessimism' retorted the French, and BAC said the Government figures were 'totally misleading'.

I chased after Benn to Paris cover more crisis talks with the French. The French gave on-the record news conferences at which they declaimed that the Concorde project must be continued. Despite Benn's announced policy of open discussions with the public about what was going on, all the British media got was assurances from public relations officers about how friendly the talks were despite 'the very difficult situation confronting us'. We also knew that Denis Healey, who as Defence Secretary had cancelled TSR2 10 years earlier, now wanted to cancel Concorde in his new post as Chancellor of the Exchequer.

With this doom-laden atmosphere exciting the BBC news desks, this time, in contrast with my first Concorde flight in Paris, there was no hesitation about laying on an expensive 'unilateral' for my TV report, in addition to half a dozen circuits for live radio discussions. Tony Benn, as he now wanted to be known, went back to London tight-lipped, sending us a message that he must report back to the Cabinet before saying anything. That did not mean that we were short of a story. The French made it clear that they accepted neither his figures nor his five options, and moreover they thought the British worried far too much about the short-term cost-effectivness of Concorde, and too little about the benefits of advanced technology that the work had already brought. They wanted to get Concorde into passenger service and see what happened then.

The Cabinet dithered, and a thousand BAC and Rolls-Royce workers marched on Whitehall when they thought that a decision was to be made in late May. That resulted in another postponement.

Chancellor Healey continued to favour cancellation. Other members of the Cabinet, probably including Benn, were inclined to accept the trade unions' advice that cancellation would cost at least £150 millions compared with the £80 millions estimated by Industry Department officials, and that if the French refused to cancel it would be wiser to go on with a limited trial in passenger service. Only the site of London's third airport, I reported, had been more bitterly divisive in Britain than Concorde.

At the end of that month Geoffrey Knight, infuriated by an overnight warning from the Department of Trade that a confidential report to the Department by British Airways stressing the unfavourable effects upon Concorde operations of 'the huge increases in aviation fuel prices', pulled off a rare public relations counter-coup. The first I knew of it was a surprise invitation from Freddie Laker to attend an important news conference a few hours later. Few public figures could have risked summoning the Press at such short notice with any confidence that they would attend in any strength. But Freddie always made big news, and the air correspondents dropped everything else and were there in force to hear him. Once again I was at the top of the main TV News:

'The Government said they wanted a public debate on Concorde. Today they got it — a public clash between British Airways and Freddie Laker, millionaire head of Laker Airways and of package holiday firms. British Airways have told the Government why they think the five Concordes they've ordered may result in losses of up to £25 millions a year, and they've asked for an assurance that they'll get a subsidy to cover those losses. Freddie Laker says that if he took over British Airways' five Concordes with the same capital support he could make a profit of £6 millions in his first year of operation and make the Concordes pay back the £155 millions they'll cost within 11 years. A special company, Concorde Air Transport, would operate them on five selected routes — all over water, with friendly Governments at the other end, and plenty of wealthy passengers . . .

'The Laker-style Concorde would get extra revenue from valuable cargo and mail, and he'd operate not from Heathrow — 'a thieves' paradise' Mr Laker calls that — but from Gatwick. Inevitably, the Laker intervention has caused embarrassment at British Airways. Several times in the past his optimistic forecasts about new British planes have proved right, and BOAC's pessimistic forecasts wrong . . .'

For the same report I interviewed Henry Marking, then Managing Director of British Airways, who riposted sourly: 'I'm a fan of Freddie Laker. But I wouldn't put my money on Freddie Laker's horses, and I wouldn't put it on his Concorde figures either.'

Afterwards I learned that Freddie had been discussing his thoughts on Concorde with Geoffrey Knight for some time previously, but had had no immediate intention of publishing them. But when Knight rang to tell him that British Airways were coming up with another 'disaster story' to support their subsidy demands, Freddie eagerly offered to publish his more positive proposals — and stole the news headlines with them.

It was July before I headed another script 'Concorde Saved Again!' reporting the French decision — accepted mutely by Britain — that production of 16 Concordes should indeed continue, keeping both production lines at Toulouse and Filton ticking over until the end of 1977. British Airways decided to speed up its entry into passenger service, and start a 500hr programme of proving flights by its pilots, which they hoped would lead to agreement on supersonic corridors through the Middle East to Japan, China and Australia. The Shah of Iran, having been flown home in a French Concorde to Tehran, announced that he would convert his three options into a firm contract.

Left: **Geoffrey Knight, vice-chairman, BAC, called in Freddie Laker to counter the unfavourable British Airways report.**

Below: **Freddie Laker to the rescue.**

Concorde 'could cost BA £25m a year'

BY LORNE BARLING

THE LATEST forecast on the operating economics of Concorde, revealed by British Airways yesterday, shows that the operation of five aircraft in a typical year would reduce profit by up to £25m.

Mr. David Nicolson, chairman of the British Airways Board, also made it clear in a letter to Mr. Peter Shore, Secretary for Trade, that the uncertainties of supersonic travel were such that they had to be underwritten by the Government.

British Airways are expecting £25m a year loss on Concorde

By Arthur Reed
Air Correspondent

In widely differing views on the cost of operating a fleet of five Concordes, British Airways yesterday expected a loss of up to £25m a year while Mr F. A. Laker, chairman of the independent airline, Laker Airways, said he could make a profit of £5,800,000.

Both estimates will be entered as evidence in the inquiry which the Government is making into whether the Anglo-French project for a 1,350 mph supersonic airliner should continue or be cancelled. The latest feeling in the British aerospace industry is that, in spite of the gloomy forecast by British Airways, which has committed itself to buy five Concordes there is now an overwhelming opinion within the Cabinet in favour of keeping the project alive.

The views of the British Airways were published in a letter from Mr David Nicolson, chairman, to Mr Shore, Secretary of State for Trade.

CONCORDE CHALLENGE BY LAKER

I could make it pay, State airline told

By PATRICK CLANCY

BRITISH Airways said yesterday that it would lose £25 million a year if it operated Concorde supersonic airliners without a subsidy.

But Mr Freddie Laker, head of the independent Laker Airways, said that his company could fly Concordes at a profit.

Prospects that foreign airlines would accept offers to lease the unsold planes had improved while the British played for time about scrapping the project; the French pressed on with another sales campaign, and invited me to travel on part of a Boston-Paris-Boston flight which was to be completed faster than a jumbo jet took to fly one way.

Although by this time I was able to introduce my broadcasts by saying that I had done more supersonic hours than any other journalist, the Paris-Boston trip was for me uniquely enjoyable.

There was no TV crew for me to serve, and for once I had time to enjoy French hospitality as well as the relaxed company of Kenneth Binning, who had taken over as the third of the British Government's Concorde 'Director Generals', provided by the Department of Trade and Industry.

We had a spare day at Boston before returning home on a 747; and he invited me to share his chauffeur-driven limousine on a visit to Cape Cod and *Mayflower II*. This is a replica of the ship which 350 years earlier, carrying 127 passengers and crew (27 more than Concorde), had taken 66 days to do the journey we accomplished in an effortless three hours; and we of course had ended where we wanted to go, whereas the *Mayflower* captain's navigation was so vague he arrived hundreds of miles from his intended destination. On the way back I drafted one of my regular pieces for FOOC:

'...My first flight in France's prototype Concorde, over three years ago, was relatively as rough and ready as the *Mayflower* voyage when compared with the sophisticated leather seats, French wines and aspic-laden food which marked the Boston crossing. Journalists' suggestions, at first rejected, that Concorde passenger cabins should have a Mach meter have now been adopted. Red computer figures flicker as speed increases — back and forth between .99 and 1.1 as the plane passes with barely a tremor through the sound barrier, 10min after take-off; then gradually rising, and taking a whole hour to reach the magic figure of Mach 2, then staying steady at 2.2, faster than a bullet, for two whole hours. For the first time Concorde was flying due west for long enough to overtake the Sun. It was 11am when we took off from Paris, with the sun streaming into our small windows from the side. By the time we arrived at Boston, it was only 9am, and the sun was coming in more weakly from the rear. Had we flown on we could have watched it sink in the East, like a film of a sunrise played backwards.

'Andre Turcat, France's austere but always courteous chief test pilot, holds court on the flight deck, half turned in his seat, explaining that he is quite free to talk, since "the workload on the pilots is not too heavy". As we burn off fuel, we float steadily upwards like a balloon to 57,000ft. "There's no need to look out of the window; there's nothing up here except U2 spy planes", he says teasingly to the *Boston Globe's* aviation editor.

'By the time we land at Boston, a sense of unity has developed between flight crew and guests, who faced the now familiar news conference together. There's an almost audible groan when, as usual, someone insists that Concorde MUST have made a sonic bang over Boston, and is quite unable to comprehend that the plane slowed far below the speed of sound long before the touchdown. Equally there's still a widespread belief that the passengers hear the sonic boom inside the cabin when the sound barrier is broken. Trubshaw and Turcat go through the regular routine of explaining that it's people on the ground — or more usually in ships — who hear a rumble as the pressure-wave caused by

110

Concorde's supersonic flight reaches the earth's surface; that *inside* the cabin you don't hear the bang, flight is much smoother, and noise level about the same as in subsonic jets . . .

'The *Boston Globe*, editorially against supersonics in this land of Senator Kennedy and Irish-Americans, likens Concorde's performance to that of a three-headed dog at a circus: you may be impressed, but don't wish to take the dog home with you. But the threatened anti-Concorde demonstrations come to nothing, and Bostonians block the roads by driving out to gaze admiringly at Concorde's sleek lines...'

I drafted that on the return flight in a scheduled-service British Airways 747, sitting beside Ken Binning in a first-class seat. He discovered that I was being mandatorily retired from the BBC staff on my 60th birthday the following year, and questioned me about my attitude to honours. 'You would be an "O" man,' he said, which I took to mean the Order of the British Empire. I failed to express enthusiasm at the prospect, and just before we touched down at 6am at Heathrow, had passed up my one and only chance of having some letters after my name and — the one aspect I regret — of providing my wife with the opportunity of going to Buckingham Palace to meet the Queen.

When the Farnborough Air Show came round again in September 1974 — it was the first fully international Farnborough, with no requirement that foreign aircraft should have British engines or components — I was able to report that for the first time for years Concorde was not the main subject of controversy. But the order book was still the subject of much speculation. With what could be claimed as 'firm' orders of two each from China and Iran (and the latter still lacked a signature) in addition to those of Britain and France, it added up to only 13. By then I talked of 'even a total of 30' being regarded as a success. George Edwards, however, in a long interview on the company's mixed prospects which we shot in the BAC chalet against the background of the well-stocked luncheon tables, insisted in his characteristic vernacular: 'So far as the civil side is concerned, we have to bash our way through the next two or three years on Concorde, which as you know is working as it should, but I frankly believe that at the end of it all we shall be selling a lot of Concordes.'

However, as the time approached for the airlines to start taking deliveries of their aircraft, British Airways (probably supported by Air France's management) made a last bid to wriggle out of responsibility for them. Henry Marking, lunching the air correspondents, expressed interest in 'a French proposal' that instead of the airlines owning their own Concordes, the British and French Governments should take over ownership of all 16 being built, place them in a pool, and lease out their flying hours — 3,000 per year per aircraft — to any airline interested. 'No', said Mr Marking, 'British Airways' interest in leasing did not mean they wanted to "welsh" on the £115 million order for five Concordes signed by them two and a half years ago.' But it was a fact that they had been unable to arrange a supersonic route to South Africa, and would have work for only four of the aircraft. Government reaction to the rent-a-Concorde plan was that it was much too late for British Airways to change their contract.

The leasing story refused to go away, however. In mid-January a private lunch with a top-level Government friend brought me an 'exclusive' story that Pan American would be operating two Concordes after all, despite being in the red financially. Negotiations were well advanced, I said in the main TV News, for

Above: **October 1975: The French Ministry of Transport at last awards its Certificate of Airworthiness.**
de Coninck

RÉPUBLIQUE FRANÇAISE

CERTIFICAT
DE NAVIGABILITÉ DE TYPE

Numéro: 78

Par le présent Certificat établi à la demande de Sociétés

S . N . I . A . S et B . A . C

*le Secrétaire Général à l'Aviation Civile soussigné, certifie que les aéronefs du (des) type(s)
désigné(s) ci-dessous satisfont par leur conception, leur définition, leur construction, leurs qualités de vol, leurs performances aux exigences des règlements de navigabilité français applicables
compte tenu des conditions d'utilisation et des limitations définies dans la fiche de navigabilité
numéro* 151 *associée au présent Certificat.*

*Ce Certificat, établi conformément aux dispositions de l'Arrêté du 6 septembre 1967
relatif aux conditions de navigabilité des aéronefs civils, est valable dans les conditions fixées
par ledit Arrêté.*

Marque: CONCORDE

Types : 1 *Approuvé le* 9 Octobre 1975

*Le Secrétaire Général
à l'Aviation Civile*

MINISTÈRE DES TRANSPORTS
SECRÉTARIAT GÉNÉRAL À L'AVIATION CIVILE

Left: **Copy of Certificate.**
de Coninck

Iran to invest over £100 millions of her oil surpluses in four Concordes, and then lease two of them to PanAm, so that, despite near-bankruptcy, the US airline need not pay for the aircraft until they were earning money. That would have the knock-on effect of causing TWA, PanAm's bitter rival, to operate a similar system with Saudi Arabia. I had a lot of detail about routes, etc, and the story caused much irritation among my rivals, for BAC said they knew nothing about it, and PanAm issued a denial in New York that any such deal had been concluded. It was an exciting story while it lasted, but alas it never happened; it could well be that my Government source hoped that it would all come true as a result of my relating it!

There followed a struggle by the airlines to obtain suitable routes on which to operate their Concordes. With no immediate prospect of the US permitting flights to New York or Washington, France negotiated one across the South Atlantic to Rio, and threatened to start operating it some months before British Airways; but this was a breach of all past agreements, and the British and French Governments put a stop to it. British Airways meanwhile, as the first leg of a planned route to Australia, were negotiating a service from London to Bahrain, but even for that said they needed supersonic corridors across Lebanon, Jordan and possibly Syria.

Sheikh Najib Almuddhin, Chairman of Middle East Airlines, always ready to needle BA, said: 'As far as I am concerned, Concorde flights can start tomorrow. I don't think the supersonic bang will worry the Lebanese. But before such flights start the British and French Governments should demonstrate their faith in Concorde by announcing that it can also fly supersonically over British and French territory.' He knew of course of Britain's earlier announcement banning such flights over Britain; so did other countries like India and Malaysia. When they were approached for overflying rights for routes to Australia and the Far East, they complained embarrassingly that they did not regard their people as second-class citizens, and rejected the requests with contempt.

It came as a relief when, in March 1975 the US Federal Aviation Administration published a 140-page 'Draft Environmental Impact Statement' recommending that, even though Concorde was 'big, noisy and dirty', the noise was not substantially higher than current subsonic jets, and it should be allowed into New York and Washington. A public inquiry was announced to hear objections.

I had my own troubles at this time. My prospects of seeing this 15-year serial story through to a successful conclusion were threatened as already mentioned by the BBC's policy at that time of mandatory retirement at 60. Programme editors wanted it to be suspended, so that I could cover the inaugural Concorde flights. But when the all-important birthday arrived on 12 May 1975, ENCA (the Editor of News and Current Affairs, Desmond Taylor) was still unrelenting; he did however finally concede that the news programmes could re-hire me on short, three-monthly contracts, and although under these I was a mere 'Special Reporter' I could continue using my Air and Defence Correspondent titles. This did have an unfortunate knock-on effect upon my inadequate pension rights — but provided the all-important immediate solution.

With relief I went off to cover the Paris Air Show a few days later, where there was even more relief in the BAC chalet when Russia's Tu-144 re-appeared, thus keeping alive their argument that the West must not allow themselves to be overtaken by the Soviet Union.

As it taxied in, amid much shouting between the ground staff and captain, who was hanging out of the open flight deck window until the Aeroflot stairs finally matched Concordski's door, a group of us were busy noting signs that the front section of the droop-snoot had recently been replaced, plus other tell-tale indications supporting rumours of technical troubles. Maybe that was why, when the captain descended, all my proffered microphone collected was a very bad-tempered 'Niet'.

Two days later however, Alexei Tupolev, designer of the Tu-144, told us that there were eight flying — matching the number of Concordes. But, he said, he had been authorised to build 20 — four more than the Concorde total. He denied the rumours of technical problems, and took us inside. Paradoxically for a Communist state, and unlike Concorde, it was a two-class plane, with ten first and 130 second-class seats. It was bigger in every way, I reported, including the windows which were much larger than Concorde's postage-stamp size. Tupolev said it would go into passenger service at about the same time, and when asked about development costs he retorted: 'Money is no problem.'

'How much will it cost to buy a Tu-144?'

'How much does Concorde cost?'

'About £24 millions.'

'Less than that!'

This was a standard example of conversation with Soviet designers, technicians and cosmonauts. I always assumed they went on courses to learn how to conduct such exchanges. It was an unhappy Air Show for the Russians. There was so much lingering resentment over the casualties caused by their crash two years earlier that they were offered only one opportunity to fly, and I believe never did take off until the plane was flown back to Moscow. But with Concorde now safe, Western interest in the Tu-144 diminished. There was a last Soviet attempt to beat Concorde into the record books by three weeks by starting regular Tu-144 supersonic services across Siberia from Christmas Day — but Aeroflot was soon forced to admit that only mail and cargo was being carried, not passengers. Increasingly after that news leaked out of the Tu-144's shortcomings — for instance that continuous use of the afterburners was needed for supersonic flying, with disastrous effects on fuel consumption and range.

In the final months before passenger services started, I was averaging one broadcast a week about Concorde. In mid-September British Concordes completed the last of 128 route-proving trials, during which 6,000 non-paying guests were carried, headed on the final flight by Dr Coggan, Archbishop of Canterbury. With happy memories of the successful opening of the Dallas-Fort Worth Airport, three members of the North Texas Commission, representing banks and big business, came to London to ask British Airways, when they got permission to fly to New York, to extend the Concorde service, subsonically if necessary, from there to Texas. They guaranteed that 40 seats would be taken on a twice-weekly Concorde service between Dallas, Washington and London.

On 9 October 1975 the French issued Concorde with their Certificate of Airworthiness, and the British Certification was issued by the Civil Aviation Authority on 5 December. There was a last flurry of Anglo-French irritation when, learning that between them BAC and British Airways were several weeks behind with their preparations, Air France said they would start their supersonic services to Rio on 4 January 1976. Eric Varley, then Industry Secretary, was

Left: **December 1975: Sir George Edwards receives Britain's Certificate of Airworthiness from, centre, Mr (later Lord) Boyd Carpenter, chairman of the Civil Aviation Authority.** *de Coninck*

Below: **Reproduction of a newspaper advertisement.**

World's first
supersonic
passenger
service

No. 7

British airways
ANNOUNCE

Wednesday, 21st January, 1976

Fly the flag.

Start of the Supersonic Era

THE FUTURE
BEGINS TODAY

Announce Reporter

BRITISH AIRWAYS introduces a new era in civil aviation this morning with the start of services for fare-paying passengers in the supersonic Concorde.

Taking off at 11.30am from London's Heathrow Airport, the airliner which cruises at 1,350 mph will streak over the 3,500 miles to Bahrain at least two hours quicker than the fastest subsonic jet — in spite of more than an hour of subsonic flight across the continent of Europe.

Businessmen in the world's major financial, industrial and commercial centres, are already viewing Concorde as an important new business tool.

Many of them are booking seats on the twice-weekly British Airways services to Bahrain, with its convenient connections to the Gulf.

Prestige flights

Departures from Heathrow have been timed to connect with incoming flights from many of the big cities in Europe and the USA. Taking the British Airways Concorde from Heathrow, at a cost of just £45 more than the normal one-way first-class fare, they will arrive at many destinations in the Gulf sooner than if they had flown direct by subsonic jet.

Concorde will help the world business community to make better use of their time, getting to their destinations fresher and more alert, while giving their companies a prestige which no other form of travel can bestow.

As Concorde climbs away from the Heathrow runway on its first scheduled service in the new supersonic era, it will be the culmination of 20 years of planning by the British aircraft industry.

It was in November 1956 that a Government committee first met to consider the feasibility of an airliner which would carry passengers in comfort at speeds up to 1,350 miles an hour.

Six years later, Britain and France signed an agreement to design, develop and manufacture such an aircraft.

5,500 hours

First flight took place on March 2, 1969, and by the time it enters service, the Concorde will be the most tested new airliner in the history of aviation.

When it received its type certificate from the Civil Aviation Authority in December, Concordes had flown a total of more than 5,500 hours, of which some 2,000 were at supersonic speeds.

British Airways has been closely associated with Concorde planning for many years. Indeed, it began

credited with persuading the French Government that after all they had been through, the two countries should stick together and start their services simultaneously. It was agreed that the French should make that possible by waiting until 21 January 1976. Lebanon and Jordan generously agreed that for the maiden flight they could be overflown supersonically, and all that remained for British Airways was to decide which 100 people should be carried on the inaugural. Alan Ponsford, public relations director of British Airways, asked my views as to who should be invited as the principal guest and I said at once 'Prince Charles', and expressed dismay when BA, told they could not have Charles, settled for the Duke of Kent. The occasion in my view, needed a superstar, and failing Charles a non-Royal figure would have been better!

Air France, having agreed to a simultaneous start for paying passengers, could not resist stealing one more march over their British rivals in the meantime — and for me it made a nice Christmas present. Having taken delivery of Concorde 205, the first fully equipped passenger version, a few days earlier, and publicly handed over a cheque in full payment for the equivalent of £26 millions, plus £16 millions for spare parts, two days before Christmas they invited one hundred French, Japanese, American and British journalists to experience the full glamour of their forthcoming service. From Paris, in a long swing over the Atlantic, we did the equivalent of a supersonic flight to New York in the time it took them to serve us with a leisurely French lunch. American travellers, I forecast, would not be able to resist it for long, whatever their own airlines did.

But I shocked my hosts by recording disappointment that French enthusiasm for the supersonic age had not been expressed with a more colourful decor. 'Beige seats with off-white walls and ceiling and a blue carpet give it a rather ordinary look. Luxurious seats, with lots of leg room by package holiday standards but definitely narrow by first-class standards.' The decor was the result of American advice, I was told rather coolly, and intended to give the aircraft 'a club atmosphere, which, as an Englishman' they thought I should appreciate. I felt a little guilty when Cyril McGhee, the airline's very Scottish UK Public Relations Manager, who enjoyed champagne and malt whisky in equal measure, wrote shortly after to welcome my participation on the 21 January inaugurals:

'May I say how much we in the Press Office appreciated your help regarding Concorde over the years, and how happy we are that due to your continual support "le jour de gloire est arrive".' There was never any matching accolade from the British; my coverage for the previous 15 years had been rather too independent to win domestic praise.

But there was one more drama to cover before the day of the inaugural. I went to Washington on 5 January to attend a somewhat bizarre 6hr hearing by the US Secretary of Transportation into applications by Air France and British Airways for amendments to their operations permits which would allow Concorde to make two daily flights each into Kennedy Airport, New York and one each into Dulles Airport, Washington. A six-man Anglo-French team, led by Ministers and civil servants was pitted against 40 objectors, who included not only US Senators and Congressmen, environmentalists and local mayors, but Britain's Bishop Montefiore of Kingston, Surrey, claiming to represent Heathrow residents — and of course Andrew Wilson.

The US Secretary proved to be William Coleman, a brilliant and formidable lawyer, and the first black man to be appointed to such high office. Gerald

116

Kaufman, just appointed as Britain's Aerospace Minister, admitted beforehand that they faced 'a formidable task'.

Kaufman caused some surprise when he said that if the case went against Concorde there would be no petty reprisals against US airlines' landing rights in Europe. Some Americans thought he had thrown away his strongest negotiating card, but it proved to be exactly the right approach so far as Coleman was concerned. Jealous of his independence he interrupted opening speeches by the British and French Ministers to seek assurances that they had no secret agreements with the US Government, for it had been widely rumoured that ex-President Nixon had promised ex-Prime Minister Heath that Concorde would be allowed in no matter how much noise it made. Kaufman said categorically that there were none; and Coleman warned the 2,000 contestants packing the auditorium that he could not please everyone, and that US airlines could lose their landing rights in Britain if bilateral agreements broke down. Charges and counter-charges became bitter as one 5min speech followed another over a period of nine hours. New York's Congressman Lester Wolff declared that Britain was so desperate to sell Concorde that she was willing to escalate the Middle East arms race by selling Jaguar strike aircraft in return for supersonic flying rights over Arab countries.

I was surprised how abhorrent it was to listen to Andrew Wilson of London's *Observer*, with whom I had worked so pleasurably for many years, say this in the witness box:

'You must be aware Mr Secretary that many people in my country are praying that you will return a negative decision on Concorde. In fact there are members of the British Government who must be hoping that you will help us to escape from the mess into which we have got ourselves by starting Concorde as a political aeroplane in 1962. We cannot ask you to repair our self-inflicted damage. But we can urge you not to damage Anglo-American relations by imposing on Americans a British aircraft that has caused anguish to everyone who has experienced its ear-shattering roar and who lives in the vicinity of its flight path.'

It was another month before Secretary Coleman rejected such urges, declared that he 'could not deny mankind this significant technological advancement' and gave permission for the Concorde services to operate for a 16-month trial period into Kennedy and Dulles Airports — although they were not permitted to fly supersonically over US territory.

Before that came 'Le Jour de Gloire' which inevitably turned out for me and most others involved to be a day of endurance rather than of glory. Only a week beforehand was Henry Marking able to take delivery from BAC of British Airways' first fully fitted-out passenger Concorde, designated, as we showed on TV News, 'Alpha Alpha', together with its flight certificate, log book and operating manuals.

The day before the inaugural the media met the nine crew members, headed by Captain Norman Todd, aged 51 and reassuringly confident with 100,000 supersonic practice miles behind him. 'It's the most beautiful aeroplane,' he said, 'but it will be a slow start. We'll fly subsonically for over 700 miles until past Venice, and go supersonic over the Adriatic . . .'

British Airways' pilots were still negotiating with the management about their supersonic pay rates — £14,000 a year compared with Air France's £42,000; and the stewardesses were unhappy about their supersonic uniforms.

Above: **21 Jan 1976: British Airways' Concorde 206 about to load passengers for the inaugural flight to Bahrain.** *de Coninck*

Below: **An inaugural passenger checking in.** *de Coninck*

Above: **More formally, the Duke of Kent follows.**   *de Coninck*

Below: **Brian Trubshaw checks in as a VIP guest on British Airways's inaugural flight.**

Only two of the six cabin crew were women and, viewed through the TV lens, contrasted with the Air France girls as having been selected (partly as a result of union pressure) for seniority and experience rather than for glamour and youthful enthusiasm. Alan Ponsford had found room for 28 out of 500 wait-listed passengers eager to pay, who would be charged £676 return, together with Mrs E Patton, who had won a ticket in a lottery in her Belfast factory. The 'VIPs' were a subtle mix of ministers, officials and trade unionists; Brian Trubshaw was there ready to help if there was trouble; and best of all there was my personal hero Group Captain Leonard Cheshire VC, the only person listed apart from the Duke of Kent who needed no explanatory designation.

In March 1959 Morien Morgan, delivering the report of the Supersonic Transport Aircraft Committee to the Ministry of Supply, had warned that delays in the research, design and development of an aircraft must be avoided, since 'they would seriously affect the competitive aspects of the aircraft.'

The Concorde project was six years late when, on Wednesday, 21 January 1976, Air France's 205 and British Airways' 206 Concordes taxi-ed out on to the Charles de Gaulle and Heathrow Airports to prepare for synchronised take-offs. Morien Morgan's warning had been overfulfilled: the arrival of Boeing's 747 jumbo Jets and the steep increases in fuel prices due to the Arab nations' fuel restrictions had not only diminished but extinguished Concorde's sales prospects.

That day however such reflections were put aside. Capt Todd had so much further to go to reach the end of the Heathrow runway that he had to start taxyng out with us seven minutes before Air France's Captain Pierre Dudal set off. Not only were the two captains in radio communication, but the two control towers were linked as well, so that they could give a simultaneous 'Clear for Take Off' at 11.32 GMT.

British and French TV networks had joined forces so that the take-offs could be watched by millions simultaneously on split screens. Europe's interest in the occasion was matched in America; and as only two camera crews could be accommodated in the BA Concorde, US correspondents from the ABC and NBC networks were sharing an NBC crew, and I was sharing an ITN crew with Peter Sissons. Having to work with an opposition crew, inevitably favouring its own correspondent, was usually a nightmare; but Peter Sissons and I had worked in friendly rivalry for years, and no one could have been more generous than Peter on such a nervy occasion. On top of that, James Wilkinson, succeeding me as BBC Radio Air Correspondent, was on board for radio, thus relieving me of another burden — but taking over, too, the most rewarding part of the occasion.

It was the first inaugural in my experience that did in fact take off on time; and soon after I transmitted a brief voice report from the flight deck for the early TV News: 'The atmosphere here on board, with the Alps showing through fleecy white cloud, is pure relief. The British and French pilots had a private agreement that, if either ran into a last minute snag, they'd wait for each other — but not for more than 20min. The Duke of Kent described our 35sec take-off as "most exciting". Henry Marking and other British Airways chiefs looked relieved when Capt Todd cut our noise by throttling back well before we left the airport boundary. For the moment all the rows are behind Concorde. Over canapés and champagne, climbing into the Sun, with the magic moment when we go through the sound barrier just ahead, Concorde's future looks bright at last.'

Above: **Leonard Cheshire VC, a Concorde enthusiast, was another inaugural guest.** *de Coninck*

Below: **The flight crew, l to r: Sr Engineer Officer John E. Lidiard; Captain Norman Todd, Captain Brian Calvert. 'A small but functional cockpit' said Calvert, who became commander on the return flight.** *British Airways*

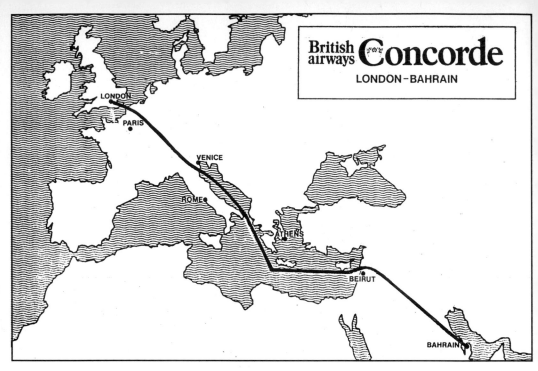

Above: **Page from brochure: The Route to Bahrain.**

Below: **Newspaper headline.**

Bahrain makes history again when Concorde lands

For nearly 5000 years of recorded history Bahrain has featured in the annals of world trade.
Now, when Concorde lands at Bahrain International Airport,
the first supersonic passenger flight to the Middle East will bridge the Gulf and Britain
—and 5000 years of international business.

In ancient times Bahrain was called Dilmun. Even then it was a great trading centre,
as the surviving texts—perhaps the world's oldest business documents—confirm.
The businessmen of antiquity chose Bahrain as their base for the same reasons as their successors of today
—a pleasant environment, swift and easy communications, a courteous and helpful people
and access to the world's most important market—now as then.

00 years ago—
rain was an earthly paradise

croak of the raven is not heard,
bird of death does not utter its cry,
ion does not devour, the wolf does
rend the lamb, the dove does not
urn, there is no widow, no sickness,
ld age, no lamentation.

m a Sumerian legend, early third
ennium BC)

00 years ago—
sinessmen were writing to one

Bahrain is a peaceful, stable land; if it
can no longer guarantee immortality it
can at present offer another blessing,
the absence of income tax for all its
fortunate inhabitants.

In 554 AD— A Bahraini poet sang
of the ship as 'the camel of the sea'

The letters of Malik's camels at dawn
appear in the broad valley of Dad like
ships in tow...which the mariner now
turns and now steers ahead; their prows
cut through the ripples as a boy divides
the sand with his hand.

(Tarafa, Bahrain's earliest known poet,
reverses the usual metaphor of the
camel being the ship of the desert.)

In 1863 AD—
Little more than a century ago, an

Ships and the sea are still a mainsta
Bahrain's economy. OAPEC's 500,0
tons drydock is being built there be
"OAPEC engaged various experts t
determine the best location...Bahra
was recommended".

I had wandered along the aisle, taking my turn with the camera crew, gathering material for use when we landed, snatching quick interviews with the Duke, Leonard Cheshire, Margaret Duchess of Argyll, and of course Mrs Patton of Bristol, for use when we arrived at Bahrain. Alas, I did not record Stanley Hooker's shout across the aisle to the Duchess when the digital machmeter in front of her refused to operate: 'Maggie, give it a bang!' he commanded; she did, and the machmeter came to life.

I had interviewed Sir George Edwards so many times in the past, that this time I left him out. It was a mistake, of course. As Kenneth Owen, in his book *Concorde: New Shape in the Sky* records, it was on this flight that he produced one of his pithiest remarks. It may have been the Duke of Kent who commented, as the Duke of Edinburgh had done before him, that supersonic flight was no different from subsonic flight. 'Yes,' said Sir George, 'that was the difficult bit.'

There was always something that one regretted not getting on tape or film. I was mulling over this as I got back to my seat when the Duke's private secretary — a Lieutenant-Commander in the Royal Navy, whose seat on the aircraft could have been put to better use — dropped into the temporarily vacant seat beside me to point out that I had breached protocol by not getting clearance from him before I leaned over Henry Marking to interview his Duke!

We curved south of Crete, passing over Lebanon well clear of Beirut, over Syria south of Damascus, across Saudi Arabia, and landed in the centre of dazzling spotlights in Bahrein, for it was already 6.45pm there, although still only 3.45pm in London. This was where my personal nightmare began. There were no colour transmission facilities from Bahrain, so a light aircraft had been chartered to fly Sissons and myself, with our cans of film, from there to Kuwait. On paper it all looked reasonable: we should take off from Bahrein 15min after Concorde landed, and the little Beechcraft would fly us 250 miles northwards up the Gulf to Kuwait City, where one of the BBC's London film editors would be waiting to process and edit our film. He would have three hours to produce an edited package for each of us, and, starting at 20.30 Sissons and I would add our commentaries during a 40min transmission period. For me there was a 30min margin for catching the 9pm news, while Peter had a much safer 90min available before News at Ten.

Of course it all went wrong. We felt we must do some filming of our arrival — the VIPs leaving Concorde, etc. Then, blinded by the searchlights we groped around in the peripheral darkness losing one another in our search for the Beechcraft.

Crammed into that without interior lights, it was impossible to work on scripts as we bumped our way apprehensively through the turbulence to descend into Kuwait's soupy atmosphere. As always, it was not fear of the flight that caused the apprehension; I think I would have welcomed a forced landing in the warm sea; the fear was of what would happen when we got to Kuwait. The worst, of course. Processing facilities hardly matched the high qualities attributed to them; and I suspect it was the first time a colour transmission by satellite had ever been attempted from there. It was 20.55 GMT — midnight in Kuwait — before we began the first attempt to transmit my story, supposed to top the 9 o'clock news. There had been no time to rehearse my script against the film, so I had to 'ad lib' as I watched the film — though I am bound to admit that I usually found that much easier than the approved method of tortuously matching three words to a second after stop-watching every shot in the film. Now each attempt was marked by some breakdown in transmission, with London telling us to stop and begin again; at 9.15pm, with the main TV News fast nearing its end, I was having one final attempt, when my monitor went black, so that I could not see the pictures being transmitted. For once my self control snapped, and I uttered a bad word — then realised that the sound was continuing. I swallowed hard, and resumed 'ad-libbing' commentary to pictures which were no longer visible but which I had at least seen several times by now, and prayed were still being transmitted:

'The space style countdown got us airborne not only on time, but in 35sec, for a flight much longer than an Atlantic crossing...As for the flight deck, I have never known it so relaxed. Behind Captain Todd, the commander, Brian Trubshaw, Concorde's chief test pilot, was taking a back seat today...Flying sub-sonically over Europe, fabulous views of the Alps...The captain warned of two slight jolts when he lit the afterburners. Just past Venice the extra thrust fired us through the sound barrier. [SOF, or Sound on Film, of Captain] That meant 23 miles a minute, faster than a bullet. At that speed, success in sight, luncheon was a cheerful affair. The cabin crew, originally worried about the narrow aisles, overcame their difficulties too [Turnill voicepiece to camera, Vox Pops, Payoff].'

I was too depressed to listen to Peter Sissons putting over his piece imme-diately afterwards — by which time the technical troubles had been overcome, giving him a reasonably clear run. Then it was back into the Beechcraft, thankful now for the darkness during the 90min of bumping back to Bahrain, and groping our way to bed in the early hours in a darkened hotel.

Later that day I was aboard Concorde's return flight to London, and *en route* pocketed the Royal Doulton bone china sugar bowl which we have used as a cream dish on our dinner table in the 18 years since then. Headwinds made our arrival nine minutes late, but there was lots of time for another TV news story that night.

They replayed for me the telecine recording of the previous night — for News had been given a few minutes of 'over-run' to insert my final transmission. The gap in my commentary, of 5-10sec, seemed to last for ever as I watched; my muffled exclamation was just audible if you listened hard; then suddenly, as I realised it was my monitor, not the film, that had failed, my commentary resumed.

It had indeed been Concorde's day of glory, dominating the world's news programmes, even though I could hardly claim that it was also mine!

CHAPTER SEVEN

Concorde's Triumph

For a few more months, I shared the confidence of many in the aviation business who believed that we would soon see the 16 production Concordes which were then either built or nearing completion operating on regular routes to the US, Australia and Japan. The French were urging Britain to agree to ordering another six Concordes, bringing the total to 22, despite the fact that their own Transport Minister, M. Cavaille, was not too happy with Secretary Coleman's decision to permit Concordes to fly to New York and Washington on a trial basis.

'It's not a real "yes" for Concorde. Not a "No". But a "yes" mixed in with conditions,' warned a dubious Cavaille. And the other question was whether Concorde operations would be allowed to start during what was expected to be at least a year of litigation by the anti-Concorde movement challenging the Coleman decision.

But when it came to operations as opposed to accountancy, British Airways was much quicker off the mark than Air France.

Henry Marking's decision to go ahead with preparations proved justified when the US aviation authorities, intimidated I suspect, by the weight of enthusiastic support for supersonics among the American public, said there was no need to delay operations while the lawyers enjoyed their Roman holiday about the issue. The first transatlantic flight carrying paying passengers was fixed for 24 May 1976 — and although by then it was one year and ten days since I had been mandatorily 'retired', thanks to the long memories and generosity of some of the Editors, and notably of Foreign Editor Larry Hodgson, I was give another short-term contract from BBC News Division to be aboard to cover it.

British Airways' preparations had included a plywood mockup with one side open — 'like a half-peeled banana' — to enable instructors to watch, so that cabin crews could be trained to give the sort of service likely to be expected by Concorde passengers who were required to pay about seven times as much for their journeys as ordinary mortals. (In the early 1990s it was ten times as much!) To give the staff some experience of 'picky' passengers, journalists were invited to take lunch in the make-believe cabin: we had caviar, prawns, oyster and pâté hors d'oeuvres, breast of chicken Jeannette, and a choice of filet of beef or lamb cutlet and duck galantine in aspic, together with salad and cheeses, followed by fresh fruit salad with kirsch or orange Grand Marnier; or fresh pineapple with rum and almonds. Wines ('Château Mouton Baron Phillipe 1970 and Chablis

Laroche et Fils 1973'); coffee, liqueurs, cigars and after-dinner mints came as a matter of course.

The need to save weight and space in the narrow passenger cabin meant that then — and now — there was no refrigerator, and dry ice was used instead. Fresh fruit was not carried, and the number of bottles, even of champagne, was kept to a minimum. But the Royal Doulton white bone china which I had admired on the Bahrain run was there, tastefully edged with interlaced gold Concordes in a dark blue background. BA had ordered 212,000 pieces, and on this inaugural I acquired — this time with the steward's permission — a pair of dainty pepper and salt containers as a lasting souvenir of this historic occasion.

What mattered then and now of course was style. In practice, the billionaire businessmen using Concorde were really interested only in the shortness of the journey; they had business lunches or dinners before or after they made it. All that many of them required during the flight was some iced mineral water to sip while they read their papers and made the decisions which were to change the lives of their tens of thousands of employees!

'Fly the Future — Fly the Flag' was the slogan produced by the advertising department when services started, with full-page advertisements in newspapers, and TV and radio spots running on British and US networks at the rate of nine a day for many weeks.

My doubts about the viability of the Concorde service to Bahrain – voiced in a TV interview and denied with a vehemence that confirmed them by a Minister who was alarmed that my suggestion would give offence to rich Arab customers – certainly did not apply to the US routes. However, airlines like Panam, TWA and Lufthansa were trying to protect their own first-class transatlantic traffic by pressuring the regulatory US authorities to push Concorde fares unacceptably high.

Because the US inaugural had far more long-term significance than the flight to Bahrain, British Airways lavished even more care and money on preparations for it — and once again the Anglo-French partnership was recognised by almost simultaneous take-offs from Paris and London. Both aircraft obviously could not land at Washington's Dulles Airport at the same time but a way was found of honouring the Anglo-French equality agreement on arrival. Air France's slightly longer route meant that its Concorde followed three minutes behind during the transatlantic crossing, and also touched down three minutes after the British plane; but then the latter deliberately spent more time taxying, so that the two Concordes finally came to a halt and cut their engines simultaneously, needle-nose to needle-nose, outside the Dulles terminal — providing a splendid spectacle for TV and newspaper photographers.

There were 35 paying passengers aboard British Airways' 3hr 40min flight, which was four hours less than the daily subsonic service operated by British Airways' 747s. The cost was £352 single compared with the subsonic first class fare of £291. The passengers included Boris Brott, principal conductor of both the BBC Welsh Symphony Orchestra and the CBC Symphony Orchestra, demonstrating how much easier his task would be in combining two jobs entailing air commuting between Canada and Wales. There was Myron Kahn, President of the Polrized Corporation of Northridge, California, who had prepared for the media a little printed note, which he filled in with times before he handed it to us, claiming that he would establish a round-trip transatlantic 'flight time' record of 10hr 10min.

24 May 1976: The British and French Concordes parked nose-to-nose at Dulles Airport at the end of the simultaneous Europe to US inaugural passenger flights. *British Aerospace*

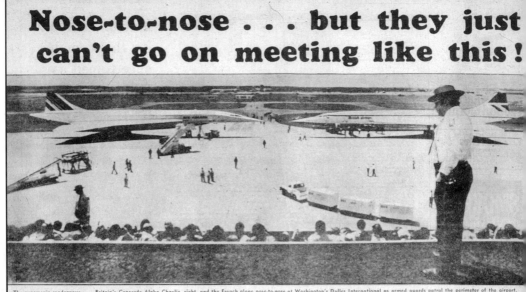

Nose-to-nose . . . but they just can't go on meeting like this!

The supersonic rendezvous . . . Britain's Concorde Alpha Charlie, right, and the French plane nose-to-nose at Washington's Dulles International as armed guards patrol the perimeter of the airport.

CONCORDE Alpha Charlie from Britain met its sister Foxtrot Alpha from France nose-to-nose on the ramp at Washington's Dulles Airport yesterday.

The supersonic age of transatlantic journeys in under four hours had arrived.

And there was hardly any sign of the fierce protest that had been feared from environmental groups in the United States.

In fact the biggest threat came from an over-enthusiastic onlooker in a light aircraft. He tried to get in on the act as the two Concordes turned in to Dulles Airport and caused a few heart-stopping moments.

As our British Airways flight, BA579 turned in banking sharply over the green Virginia fields, we could see in the heat haze the Air France plane banking to follow to three miles instead.

Ignored requests

FROM ANGUS MACPHERSON WHO WAS ON BA 579'S TRAIL-BLAZING FLIGHT

ignored requests from the authorities to keep away. It was not a near miss and we shall not be making a report.

It was the only thing that disturbed the fantastically smooth operation that had whisked us from London to Washington in 3hr 52min.

Only two line protesters stood out against the triumphal welcome.

At Heathrow before we left the head of the anti-Concorde protest, the tall bearded figure of Richard Wiggs could be seen on the VIP walk-in to the Concorde lounge, offering leaflets to passengers urging them not to fly on the supersonic plane.

He was warned by police that he was breaking an airport bylaw, but a compromise was eventually reached. He was

Why do you want to damage the environment?

Before take-off British Airways pilot Brian Calvert welcomed us aboard the flight—'the first time the brave little bird has been allowed to go to America,' he said.

Then, bang-on time at one minute past one, he opened the throttles of the four Rolls-Royce engines and Concorde slid into the air—a shade heavily—for its first fully representative passenger flight across the Atlantic.

At 1.28 over the Bristol Channel south of Barry the throttles opened again in escape us through the sound barrier. At 2 p.m. we were at our full cruising speed of 1,350 m.p.h.—twice as fast as sound.

Just before 4.0, after a spectacular view of Cape Cod, Concorde slowed down

But the technological superlatives were not really the point any more.

Now the paying passengers—there were 16 among the 76 travellers on board —will have their say at £233 a time. That is the price of a single fare whether the £1,390 million Anglo-French venture succeeds or fails depends on their enthusiasm or rejection.

Judging by yesterday's reactions, they are high hopes of success. Almost everyone on board was enthusiastic.

John Trotter, a 58-year-old Edinburgh bus conductor, who spends most of his working day on a 32-minute run from Edinburgh to the village of Balerno, had no doubts at all.

'It's absolutely marvellous — worth all the money,' he said.

'I've been waiting for this since June 1946, when I put my name down for a ticket. Flying is my hobby. I don't smoke. I don't drink. I'm not married and I had just one ambition — to ride on Concorde.'

Commuter boon

A conductor of a different sort, Boris

The sight that mad a whole town gasp

From WILLIAM LOWTHER in Herndon, Virginia

IT WAS just before high noon on the main street in Herndon and the whole town had turned out to hear Concorde.

But after first the British Airways plane flew over and then the Air France it was the sight and not the sound that made them gasp.

'They were just fantastic. Why, even seeing them gives you the gooce bumps,' said Cathy Jarvis, who dished from her office switchboard out on to the street when she first heard

'Of course we'll have wait until we hear a Cr off. But we all had making family lunch to planes.'

'It wasn't that noi all,' said Mrs Joyce Gre who left off making family lunch to see planes.

soric perhaps more t anywhere else in nation. They are so that it might make already had more noise unbearable.

But the fears were back yesterday in the of reality.

Above: **24 May 1976: The** *Daily Mail* **records the nose-to-nose arrival at Washington's Dulles Airport at the end of the inaugural transatlantic passenger flight.**

Left: **Souvenirs of the first flight.** *Graham Turnill*

He had caught the overnight jumbo jet from New York, giving him four hours in London to sign a big contract before catching Concorde to fly back again. 'This first commercial supersonic flight to the United States is particularly exciting to me, since I still recall using a horse and buggy,' said his note — which of course invited us to interview him. There was John Trotter, a 58-year old Edinburgh bus conductor, who boasted of having flown 110,000 miles, with the supersonic flight fulfilling his supreme ambition. Five people had won tickets in a Currys Ltd competition, and another married couple had won a *Daily Mail* competition. All-important on such an occasion was Henry Murray, whose luggage was crammed with Concorde envelopes — 'first day covers' — franked with special commemorative postmarks.

There were 26 of us 'media' representatives, with just one female among us — young Lesley Judd, beginning her TV career as a BBC Blue Peter presenter, with the nerve-wracking job of doing a live report by satellite ahead of the rest of us into that evening's programme. (I gave her what help I could, but she did not need much!) Peter Sissons was there again for ITN, as always a pleasant rival, with no hint of the highly-paid stardom he was to achieve on BBC Television News a few years later.

Compared with the Bahrain inaugural, it was a luxurious trip for us; since there was live TV coverage of both our departure and arrival we had no camera crew flying with us; and BBC Radio was again being covered by James Wilkinson, so all I had to worry about was one report into the TV 'unilateral' after Lesley had done her piece. I was still, however, so 'programmed' for continuous high-pressure work, that I felt somewhat lost.

British Government representation on the flight was not strong. One suspected deep-rooted resentment that Concorde still existed, and Edmund Dell, Secretary of State for Trade, pulled out a day beforehand, leaving the job to the junior minister, Gerald Kaufman. Under Secretary Ken Binning was there, however; a powerful and enthusiastic civil servant. We had to manage without a Royal presence, thus escaping the accompanying penalty of providing seats for the hangers-on.

On every seat when we entered the plane there was an Oxford-blue folder, embossed in gold 'British Airways' and carrying the legend 'Inaugural flight of the first North Atlantic scheduled supersonic passenger service. 24 May 1976. BA579. London Heathrow Airport to Washington DC'. I carefully filed it, and found it with difficulty 14 years later, when searching for material for this book.

It contained lists of passengers, flight times showing that it was 36 minutes after take-off, passing Porthcawl, before we began to accelerate, and carefully NOT mentioning just where we broke the sound barrier; biographies of the crew and stewards — a total of nine men; and an envelope containing souvenirs. They included a leather name-tag for luggage with such large Concorde symbols one dared not use it because it was such a temptation to souvenir hunters; a leather wallet to protect one's passport; and a small brochure entitled 'Your 23-mile-a-minute fact sheet'. In that was a photograph of a businessman passenger using a pocket calculator; for them the computer age was just beginning! A handout eulogised the menu — 'From Caviar to Camembert'.

In Washington the transmission facilities, organised by the BBC office and partly financed by Children's Programmes for Lesley Judd, were as perfect as I have known them before or since. The expensive 'satellite-throw' even had autocue facilities so that for once I could look like a calm professional, unimpaired by lack of sleep, pronouncing impartial judgements into TV News:

'"Concorde is almost through the barrier of public acceptibility"'. That's how Henry Marking, British Airways' managing director, summed up what appeared to us passengers to be a rapturous reception. Mr Marking had flown in here from Australia — where he'd apparently been given assurances that next year Concorde services can be extended from Washington here, right through London, to Bahrain, Singapore and Melbourne.

'Of our 76 passengers, 40 were VIPs and newsmen. The rest paid £352 per head for the one-way flight. One of them, John Boothroyd of Sheffield, booked his flight in 1962, the day Julian Amery, then Aviation Minister, signed the Anglo-French Concorde Treaty. On board today Mr Amery told me he'd insisted on a "no-break" clause in the Treaty because he thought the French might want to back out. "I never thought it would be the British who'd try to back out," he said. "But I'm very glad I put it in."

'What comes next? Not the 300 Concorde orders once so confidently forecast. But the British and French planemakers hope that Pan American and TWA, with their first-class traffic threatened, will either buy or lease enough Concordes to keep the production lines ticking over for the next 10 years. Even 20 or 30 orders will enable Rolls-Royce and BAC to develop what's now known as Concorde 1A. Improved wings and quieter engines would be developed on a pre-production Concorde now scheduled for the scrap heap at the end of this year. Cost — about £50 millions. But until there are more Concorde orders the Government, I was told today, will continue to be sceptical.'

That was almost the end of my first-hand coverage of the long-running Concorde saga, because I became more and more immersed in space coverage, and in the creation and annual publication of *Jane's Spaceflight Directory*, which grew to a 600-page, 600,000-words monster, weighing down my working life. So it was with some concern that I observed that whereas the Russians, fighting back, announced that they had started scheduled passenger services from Moscow to Alma Ata on 1 November 1977, British Airways' attempts to extend the London-Bahrain service to Singapore had to be suspended in December 1977, after only three flights. Malaysia imposed an overflying ban, for reasons which only those directly involved understood — but which I suspect involved Malaysian resentment at what they felt was the superior attitude of our diplomats coupled with assumptions that supersonic overflight of their territory should be permitted when it was completely banned in Britain. Prolonged inter-Government talks followed, and over a year later, on 24 January 1979, the service was resumed on a joint British Airways/Singapore Airlines basis. Permission had been given for supersonic flight along the Malaccan Straits — 'an extremely good route, and great fun to fly' Captain John Hutchinson told me. 'We could accelerate up the Straits, be supersonic 11-12min after take-off, and continue supersonically virtually all the way to Bahrain.' But less than two years later, on 1 November 1980, the route had to be abandoned.

Politics had intervened — partly because of the offence caused by an ITV programme called 'Death of a Princess'. Saudi Arabia withdrew permission for supersonic flight over the Empty Quarter, first saying it was becoming more inhabited, and then that it was a danger area due to their own military flying operations.

130

DULLES INTERNATIONAL AIRPORT

DATE: May 25, 1976

South Operation

REVISED   Preliminary Take-Off Noise Data

Aircraft	Take-off Point Approx. 3.5 nm	1500 feet**
DC-8	109 to 112 PNdB	
B-707	113 PNdB	
AF Concorde	129 PNdB	
4 Engine Jet	99 PNdB	
B-707	102 PNdB	
B-707	111 PNdB	
BA Concorde		96 PNdB**

* Due to pilot request for change of Runway, mobile monitoring
    equipment not in the same position for take-off monitoring.

** 1500 feet east of centerline about 24,000 feet (approx. 4
    nautical miles from brake release

These values are maximum Perceived Noise Levels in PNdB units.
This is the unit used at Heathrow, Charles DeGaulle and JFK for
noise monitoring.

The Effective Perceived Noise Levels in EPNdB units, used for
FAA noise certification and specified in the Environmental
Impact Statement, are obtained by processing the tape recording
through a computer. These values will be available as soon as
possible.

US noise data on the Dulles take-off tests.

In the meantime Concorde 216, the last off the two production lines, had made its maiden flight from Filton on 20 April that year. The transatlantic services operated by France and Britain flourished, but British Airways' subsonic extension, under the Braniff flag, had to be abandoned as uneconomic only 17 months after being started on 12 January 1979 — one reason being that Concorde consumed fuel at the same rate when flying subsonically as supersonically. Since only half the distance was covered subsonic, fuel costs were doubled.

The final abandonment of the sales campaigns upon which so much enthusiasm and money had been spent came on 21 September 1979 with a joint Anglo-French government announcement that the unsold aircraft and their support engines would be shared between Air France and British Airways. British Aerospace and Aerospatiale each retained one production aircraft, so that meant a total of seven each for the two national airlines.

By now, what the Soviets were achieving with the Tu-144 had become academic — and it was quite difficult to find out, anyway.

However, Aeroflot finally admitted that only 102 Moscow-Alma Ata passenger flights were made before this service was suspended following a crash involving a Tu-144 on a non-commercial flight. A much-improved version of the aircraft, the Tu-144D, appeared in mid-1979, and in 1981 Soviet Ministry of Aircraft Production officials were still saying that 'it could soon be back in service'. But it never was, and presumably the 15 completed 'Concordskis' out of the total 75 planned, have long since been scrapped.

For Concorde too the early 1980s were years of retrenchment: Air France had to abandon its services to Caracas and Rio because of heavy losses, and British Airways' Bahrain service finally collapsed as the prospects of continuing the route to the Far East diminished.

Since then, however, with Concorde's qualities and limitations equally recognised and accepted, the world's most advanced aircraft continued to perform with near-perfection. After five years in service the fleet had made over 15,000 flights and carried 700,000 passengers.

Even the political quarrels finally petered out. The House of Commons Industry and Trade Committee held periodic inquiries into costs, and complained that the project 'had acquired a life of its own and was out of control'. Such complaints died out when in 1983 British Airways said they no longer needed the subsidy they had demanded to operate Concorde. Some final bickering as to whether France or Britain had paid more than their fair share of the development and production costs was also settled, and the joint project officially concluded. Any lingering irritation over these little differences was of minor importance when measured against the fact that successful collaboration had been achieved between the two countries, overcoming the formidable historic barriers of different languages and systems of measurement.

From then on, aerospace collaboration continued on civil projects like the Airbus regardless of divergences between the two Governments.

I came back into the story in April, 1989, when radio and TV programmes wanted to mark the 20th anniversary of Concorde 002's maiden flight in Britain. This was a pleasure, because at last the interest was not in the political failures but in the flying success of a beautiful aeroplane. BBC Radio Bristol arranged for 002's original flight crew to gather again on its flight deck in the Yeovilton Museum so their reporter Roger Bennett could interview them and me, and to

Most of the 16 production Concordes appear at an advanced stage of construction in these pictures. *British Aerospace*

enable me do a piece for Breakfast TV. Margaret and I had a rewarding two days' driving from Yeovilton to Brian Trubshaw's home in Wiltshire and then back to his former headquarters at Weybridge to interview Sir George Edwards.

Miraculously the Breakfast TV story was ready for transmission on the right day, 20 years after 001's first flight: 'Engineers, designers, airline pilots and aviation experts are gathering in Toulouse to celebrate the 20th anniversary of Concorde,' said the beautiful girl presenter. 'The supersonic jet, a miracle of its age back in 1969, has been at the centre of bitter debate ever since. To some a technological masterpiece, to others a rich man's plaything. But while fears over the safety of air travel have reached new heights, Concorde has an unblemished safety record.'

My report started with some film of 001's first flight, and a clip of Turcat telling me after landing: 'We had no actual troubles — only the weather.' I pointed out that it was six years after the maiden flights before Concorde started carrying passengers. As I emerged from 002, 'now just a museum piece', I patted its fuselage affectionately and did my party piece to the camera: 'Covering the Concorde story was a real pain. Everybody was always quarrelling about it, especially the British and French governments, with the French of course usually getting the best of it. Everybody inside as well as outside the BBC expected me to knock Concorde, but I always felt that British industry would die unless it had advanced technological projects like this...The man who had to make Concorde work against that awful background of political squabbles was Chief Test Pilot Brian Trubshaw.'

The Breakfast TV producer, like all producers, wanted his piece to look different. So instead of interviewing Trubshaw there and then in Concorde, we went off to his home, where we arrived late in the evening. For some reason I cannot remember we entered his rather remote country house by a side door, and five of us, loaded with gear, tramped into the lounge unannounced. Mrs Trubshaw was convinced she was being invaded by burglars, and it was some minutes before Brian, who had let us in and then gone off on some errand, could be found to vouch for us. TV camera crews on location tend to dress for protection against eventualities rather than for sartorial elegance!

We introduced Brian over close-ups of some of his trophies, zooming in to a colour photo of the whole Concorde support team, and then he was found picking up from my commentary: 'It didn't make life any easier, the fact that people doing my side of the business were well aware that there were a number of other people trying to cancel the project at fairly frequent intervals. But I think in some ways it made those of us intimately involved more determined than ever. And certainly we really believed that it could be made to work. An awful lot was learned from Concorde. The fact that the British and French could get together and form a team to do a job like this — that in itself was a fairly tremendous thing. A lot of the knowledge on structures, advanced aerodynamics and the propulsion system has all been put to good use in other areas.'

'Only 16 passenger Concordes were built', I continued over black and white film of assembly work. 'Production ended when the world's airlines refused to buy them. Even British Airways and Air France demanded subsidies before they would take them — though today they are earning handsome profits. Sir George Edwards, now in his eighties, looks back on its wonderful success as one of his most frustrating tasks.'

134

Sir George then walked into shot, jaunty as ever, wearing the same old pork-pie trilby which in 30 years he had never failed to sport when in the public eye, as he showed me around his old Weybridge headquarters among the now deserted aircraft hangars: 'I used a lot of the best years of me life beating me brains out on the programme in the face of great difficulties from the administration point of view. Technically it was a good job, and it stands up in comparison with anybody in the world because nobody yet has done it. Several people had a cut at it, including the Russians — and the Americans' efforts at it were absolute comic relief.'

In my payoff I repeated my proud claim to have clocked up more than 100 hours flying on Concordes. 'For me it was a miracle. Travelling at twice the speed of sound, approaching 1,400mph, finally beats that awful jet lag. You arrive in New York two hours before leaving London.' Fortuitously a schoolteacher arrived, escorting her class of knowledgeable seven-year olds through 001. The BBC cameraman moved smoothly in among them; and over shots of small boys crowding quizzically into the flight deck I concluded:

'But Concorde's life is limited. It could last to the year 2000 — but already tomorrow's passengers are thinking about spaceplanes.'

This of course has proved not to be true. My final chapter tells how Britain took the lead in organising a seven-nation study of what sort of aircraft should follow Concorde, and it is much more likely to resemble a larger version of Concorde than a spaceplane.

Although I said in my valedictory TV piece that covering Concorde had been 'a pain', there are of course moments and memories in the saga that I cherish. One of these was sharing a satisfying lunch of sausages and baked beans in the Yeovilton Museum canteen with Messrs Trubshaw, Cochrane and Watts, after we had completed our interviews in 002. While they reminisced I learned more about the traumas and emergencies that they had faced and overcome during the development programme. The guilty twinges suffered by my journalistic conscience because John Cochrane was seldom interviewed or even mentioned during that time were reinforced. All the news and current affairs programmes expected to see and hear Brian Trubshaw because he was 'No 1', and they would have been offended at being offered his deputy, John Cochrane. But by the end of the test flying programme, because Brian got caught up in politics and administration, John had done at least as much of the development work — and as Brian pointed out earlier, Cochrane also did much of the hazardous flying required before the engine surge problem was cured. It was John's flying skill too which averted a major crash after 002 had given a demonstration flight at an Air Day at Weston-super-Mare in August 1974.

Another test pilot had taken over the left-hand seat for the return to Fairford and had selected 'landing gear down' with the aircraft banked at 45° and halfway around a turn. That was followed by two loud bangs and a violent structural impact. The Flight Engineer, carrying out an inspection from a hatch in the cabin floor, discovered that the left-hand leg was down but unsupported. Releasing the undercarriage during the turn had resulted in it descending in a 'free-fall' and causing much damage.

A full emergency was declared, police rushed to close the perimeter roads around Fairford, John resumed his place in the left-hand commander's seat, and

Above: **August 1975: Actor Robert Morley and Douglas Bader enjoy a PR flight on Concorde with Flight Director Jimmy Andrews.** *de Coninck*

Below: **002's original test flight crew reassembles with the prototype, now on display at Yeovilton, in April 1989.**

Above: **April 1989: Sir George Edwards recalls the Concorde battles at his former Weybridge HQ. All that remains there now is the museum.**

Left: **John Cochrane, BAC test pilot, who did much of the hazardous flight testing required to cure surge problems when throttling back from supersonic speeds.** *de Coninck*

nursed 002 down to a gentle landing with the aircraft rolled so that at touch-down most of the weight was on the right-hand undercarriage leg. Delicate use of the braking parachute and reverse thrust brought it to a stop; but with the aircraft in imminent danger of collapsing on to its fuselage, the seven man crew made a hurried exit through the emergency hatch over the right wing. Ground personnel rushed to get jacks under the aircraft before it collapsed — and succeeded. Whether or not the test pilot had been in error in lowering the under-carriage during a turn, a design deficiency had been exposed, and the French manufacturer of the undercarriage modified it accordingly. Had the weakness not been found until Concorde was in service with 100 passengers aboard, the result would undoubtedly have been much less happy.

John Cochrane was involved in a more public drama when training British Airways' crews during the intensive five months' route-proving phase with one of the production Concordes.

'It was very unfortunate, to put it mildly,' he told me. 'Due to a little bit of confusion on the flight deck when we were flying between London and Bahrain, we dropped what you might call a massive boom over Beirut. We were sup-posed to decelerate from Mach 2 at the eastern end of the Mediterranean just after we had gone left-hand down a bit past Cyprus, so that we were subsonic before we crossed Beirut. But the Flight Engineer had got his checklist upside down — and let me hasten to say it wasn't Brian Watts but a BA chap — and we were still supersonic when we arrived over Beirut. I realised we had been a bit late, but hoped it was not too obvious. However, when we landed in Bahrain I was told I had started a war in Beirut, because the boom had been taken by some sections of the communities there to be the start of hostilities.

'Brian Trubshaw doesn't like to be reminded of this, but he grounded me there until he arrived to fight my corner for me — for which I was thankful, for they were talking of shipping me back to Beirut to answer personally for what had happened — in which case I would probably still be there! It showed how difficult it was to operate an aeroplane of this capability in an environment which was not quite ready to accept it.'

As Concorde work tailed off into mere maintenance, Brian Trubshaw was made Director and General Manager of British Aerospace's Filton Division until he retired, properly loaded with international medals and trophies at the age of 62 in 1986. He then became a valued member of the Civil Aviation Authority, which makes Britain's flying rules and sets safety standards which are respected around the world. John Cochrane was not quite so lucky. With little test flying left for him to do, he decided to leave British Aerospace and went back to work as a civil airline pilot. When we met at Yeovilton he was flying the A320 Airbus for Cyprus Airways, with a home in the sunshine there as well as one in Britain, and assured me that he and his family loved their much more routine life.

I have always been struck by the way that all the people responsible for developing Concorde speak of it not as an aircraft or a plane or a jet, but as 'the aeroplane'. Their respect for this superb denizen of the stratosphere is now shared by more than three million passengers, as well as most of the millions living below its flight path. New passengers continue to be captivated by its quality, while those living beneath its flight path, even when irritated by its distinctive noise, gaze up with admiration as 'the aeroplane' passes safely overhead.

138

CHAPTER EIGHT

Concorde's Happy Ending

In aviation especially one never tempts fate by boasting about safety records. But at the time of writing the Anglo-French supersonic aeroplane has performed superbly for nearly 25 years since its maiden flight on 2 March 1969. Having spent most of the time on flights from London to Washington and back from New York in January 1993 in the fourth crew seat, I could appreciate Captain John Hutchinson's assessment: 'It's a very strong, very robust aeroplane, delightful to fly, precise, with terrific power, and very responsive. But it will make a fool of you very quickly if you don't treat it properly.'

I saw for myself the truth of his statment that 'there's a good workload on the flight deck.' Pilot, co-pilot and flight engineer were all concentrated upon pre-flight, pre-landing and post-landing checklists, as well as upon noise and boom control procedures: 'Three, two, one, *noise*!' called the captain a minute after take-off; throttles were eased back by the flight engineer and switches thrown by the co-pilot. They were of course lowering, not increasing the noise being generated outside the airport as we climbed towards cruising height.

When he retired just before talking to me John Hutchinson had clocked up more hours on Concorde flight decks than anybody else — 5,500, of which 3,000 were supersonic, a record unattainable by any military pilot either now or in the foreseeable future.

It is because you are covering the distance in half the time — we did the London-Washington flight in 3hr 40min against headwinds of up to 70mph, and New York-London with strong tailwinds in 3hr 5min — that there's a good workload on the flight deck. 'In a way I think that's going to be the problem with the planes of the future,' says John. 'Not enough workload. It's all becoming so automated there's nothing for the pilots to do, and that worries me. As long as you have human beings on the flight deck you need to give them a job to do, otherwise . . .'

The in-service reliability of Concorde is officially given as 4-5% worse than that of subsonic aircraft, but considering that it was designed in the mid-1960s,

All that remains of America's $1 billion effort to match Concorde with a rival supersonic airliner: While covering the Space Shuttle Mission to repair the Hubble Space Telescope in December 1993, the author stumbled upon the fuselage of the full-size feasibility mockup of the Boeing 2707 mouldering away in a junkyard five miles from the entrance to the Kennedy Space Center in Florida.

Weeds grow between the three sections of the fuselage. A protective tarpaulin has rotted away to disclose, below the flight deck window, the insignia of 22 airlines, including BOAC, who matched their provisional Concorde orders with at least equivalent orders for the B2707.

For most of the quarter-century since the project was abandoned the mockup has been displayed in museums. But recently, apparently, it was thought to be occupying more room than interest in it justified – hence its removal to the junkyard.

and as John puts it is 'still at least 20 years ahead of its time' that is astonishingly good.

Captain Dave Leney, another recently retired Concorde pilot, who also helped me with the final stages of this book, supplemented this: 'Concorde is like all planes: they need to be used all the time, and then they work. One of the major problems we had was with the hydraulics a few years ago, and that was because it was left sitting in freezing weather overnight in New York.' Heat the aircraft can tolerate, for its fuselage of aluminium alloy, with some steel and titanium near the engines, is designed to withstand being 'cooked' during supersonic cruise at over 90°C, rising to 127°C on the nose.

Three times Concorde failures have been in the news when they have lost part of the rudder during flight, but while vibration in the rear of the two passenger cabins causing the champagne glasses to rattle did alarm the passengers, landing was no problem. The failure was due to corrosion debonding the outer skin from the rudder's internal honeycomb structure, and not the result of any structural weakness. Redesigning the rudders, together with a general refurbishment of the British Airways Concorde fleet inside and out at a cost of several million pounds has served to reassure the pilots and technical staff and convince the airline's accountant-managers that it makes financial sense to keep the fleet flying for another 10 to 15 years.

I made my flights — by courtesy of British Airways — because I had not had any personal experience of Concorde since the historic inaugurals in 1976-77. I wanted to experience the reaction to what is now a routine service of passengers and pilots who had no experience and little knowledge of all the aggravation that I had reported. Most passengers, if they can afford the bruisingly high fare — or, more likely, offset the £5,100 cost against tax on very high earnings — become addicted to using Concorde. A daytime flight back from the US, instead of aboard one of those appallingly crowded 'red-eye' night flights in jumbo jets, was a luxury indeed. Including three hours' driving time to and from the airports, a subsonic flight from Washington to New York, and a two-hour wait there (in the Concorde lounge), the journey home took me 11 hours, at an average speed of about 360 mph; and as my 'day' was five hours shorter than usual, bedtime came around earlier, and I got up next day with no jet lag.

In mid-January we were very lightly loaded, with only 45 passengers on the outward flight and 39 on the way back; the average load is 60 in 100 seats, so most passengers routinely get the use of two seats — especially if they are physically bulky. It is rare to see anyone sleeping on Concorde; usually they are busy studying their briefs and tapping their laptop computers, or immersed in business talks. But it must be admitted that not all are happy with Concorde's narrow tube-interior. One large, bearded passenger, whom I at first mistook for Pavarotti, told a stewardess in vigorous language that he was most unimpressed. I suspect he had had a close encounter with the toilets, which are cramped even by comparison with those in charter-holiday jets. An effort has been made to make shaving possible by providing a let-down table-top over the toilet seat; but the hand-basin is minute, the hot water variable, and the divided door, which must be pushed or pulled inwards, can jam if handled roughly, and a bulky person has problems getting out. But the flights are so short that the regular Concorde user avoids the need for inflight toilet encounters!

I confess I was slightly embarrassed to find myself seated beside 'Ted E Bear', sent on an around-the-world trip by Class 3B at Rice Elementary School at Conroe, Texas. Airlines apparently collaborate occasionally in such projects, passing the teddy from one airline to another, and recording details in an accompanying logbook. I soon got over the shock, and added my own entry for the benefit of the students. I hope that Anglo-American relationships may as a result be a few degress warmer when one of them achieves high office on Capitol Hill.

Flight deck announcements are made almost unnecessary by the digital machmeters above the front seat rows in each cabin giving, on the left side, the speed and altitude (Mach 2, 50,000ft), and on the other side temperature and distances ('-61°C, MPH 1,220', or alternatively 'Miles to Go 3,080'). Only *aficionados* appreciate the subtleties of these figures: while the pilot keeps the Mach speed steady at two, outside temperature changes cause the speed to vary by as much as 100 mph; and as Concorde burns off its fuel it floats upwards; the altitude gradually increases from 50,000 to perhaps 58,000ft — 'cruise climb', the pilots call it.

A disappointment is that it is difficult to photograph the green, computer-generated figures on the machmeters; it needs good film and a smart photographer to persuade them to register. 'Freebies' for the passenger in addition to the attentive service of champagne and wine — frequently rejected by the businessmen in favour of mineral water — include a 12.5 x 9in soft leather wallet, containing leaflets and a beautiful stainless steel Concorde pen; a steward also delivered a 'personal gift' which proved to be a hip flask on the outward journey, and on return a leather wallet for credit and business cards — 'A reminder of your flight on board Concorde, the Flagship of the British Airways fleet and the ultimate in air travel'. I was given an independent estimate that these giveaways must cost £50 per passenger — and on a half-empty plane some passengers collect three or four wallets with their prestigious contents to give to their relatives and children.

Only the wealthy could be expected to patronise the 'Concorde Duty Free Selection'. Perfumes range from Escada at £39 for 7.5ml to Ralph Lauren Safari at £120 for 15ml; a Hermes silk scarf is £99.50 (it is described as 'the ultimate Parisian accessory', and I bought one of these for my wife, thinking it was priced in dollars).

Other offerings include a Mikimoto cultured pearl brooch at £325 and Raymond Weil Gloria watches — £349 for a lady and £369 for a gentleman. Glenmorangie Malt Whisky ('a limited edition of unique vintage' dated 21 January 1976) was offered at £150 for 75cl, fountain pens at £225 and £375, ties at £42 and £27, and the cheapest offering was a Concorde Stick Pin at £11.50.

I did not see anybody else buying these luxuries, but then I was fortunate in being invited to spend most of my time on the flight deck. There you quickly become aware that a pilot's life on Concorde is even more addictive than that of pilots on other aircraft. David Leney had already told me how, when he had to retire as a Concorde commander, he bid successfully for a place as co-pilot, and added two extra years to his supersonic career on British Airways' transatlantic routes by transferring to the right-hand seat. Capt Colin Morris, in command on my outward flight, shared Leney's intention to continue flying Concorde just as long as he was allowed to — and was ready to move into the right-hand seat if

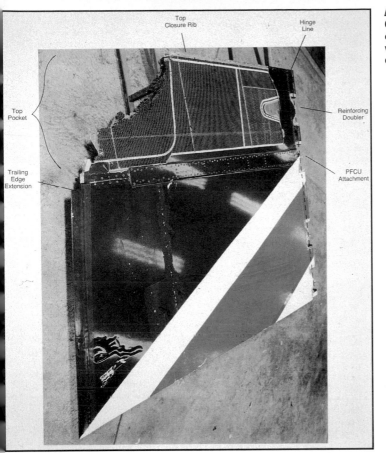

Top Closure Rib

Hinge Line

Top Pocket

Reinforcing Doubler

Trailing Edge Extension

PFCU Attachment

Left: **Three times Concordes have lost part of the rudder during flight, with no serious consequences.**

Below: **January 1993: Flight deck on a New York-London flight. Left to right: Capt Mussett, First Officer Graham, Flt Eng Quarry.** *R. Turnill*

Left: An unsual transatlantic passenger — manifested as Ted E. Bear flying around the world as part of a Texas school project. His log book is also on the seat.

Below: Concorde test pilots are still in demand for lectures and awards. Here Brian Trubshaw receives the Captain Barnwell Trophy from Peter Calder, who was Rolls-Royce's Chief Development Engineer on the Olympus engines.

younger pilots eager for promotion succeeded in displacing him in the commander's seat.

He was a bit surprised when I asked him if he felt he was flying a 'vintage' aeroplane. 'It may be ancient in that basically it was designed that long ago,' he said, 'but it's still doing a job which is unsurpassed in aviation. Just because it's not a "glass cockpit" doesn't necessarily date it. The glass cockpit (pilots' jargon for a cockpit with screens instead of dials and switches) is only a cheaper way of providing the information, and may be a little bit more efficient. But on the other hand we have a lot more information available to us to make decisions and to manage the aircraft systems and to salvage things when they are going wrong. We get all the information all the time; you can see trends on it, whereas with a glass cockpit I rather fancy you only get the information when it actually starts to go wrong and comes up on the screen for you.

When I suggested that it was a happy coincidence that flying Concorde was one of the highest paid jobs in the aviation business Colin Morris was visibly shocked. 'Who have you been talking to?' he demanded. 'Would that it were true. We don't fly Concorde for money. If we were going to do that we would be scrambling to get on the Boeing 747-400. We come to Concorde for the love of flying, the love of the aeroplane, and the lifestyle. In the early days the Concorde captain was actually paid quite well, but it has gradually been eroded, probably because we are not a very large group, and don't have a very large voice, and if people were honest they could see we were having rather a good time and don't deserve money as well.'

In fact all British Airways' senior captains get the same basic salary — about £60,000 at the time of writing. However, the system of allowances associated with different aircraft types and routes results in substantial differences in final pay rates, making it much more profitable to fly the latest jumbo jets — the Boeing 747-400s. The 'bidding system' which enables senior captains to select the most favourable routes enables some of them to earn nearer £100,000 a year, and one suspects that this also applies to some Concorde pilots.

As we prepared to pull back from the gate at Kennedy at the start of my return journey, this time with Captain Geoffrey Mussett in command, but with First Officer John Graham once again in the co-pilot's seat, we had to pause while Captain Morris parked the arriving Concorde from London alongside. Kennedy Airport Control were always helpful, I was told, but Concorde got no priority when it came to lining up for a take-off slot, and we had to wait while a squat little Shorts' Skyvan moved in between us and the queue of six jumbo jets and airbuses ahead of us. Because we were so lightly loaded the cabin crew had asked some of the passengers to move from the rear into the forward cabin, and in due course we climbed past the tip of Long Island to level off at 9,000ft and a speed of Mach 0.95. Within minutes permission came to climb to 30,000ft and from there we 'transitioned' from subsonic to supersonic flight, at the same time climbing on to 50,000ft.

During this time, as our speed moved up through the sound barrier (and I could detect no jolt as I did on the prototypes) to Mach 1.4, the aircraft's centre of gravity moved rearward — the reason for asking the passengers to move forward — and powerful pumps transferred fuel imperceptibly from forward to rear tanks. 'Standby Reheats' said Captain Mussett, and with John Graham and Terry Quarry the Flight Engineer (on almost his last flight before retiring) there

145

was fierce concentration on throttles, dials and switches as the engine afterburners were switched on in pairs. This maximum use of power cannot be employed for more than 15min; but in only 10min 2sec our speed had risen to Mach 1.7, from which normal engine power took us smoothly on to Mach 2 cruising speed. We reached that in 31min 10sec from take-off, and from then on Concorde's tendency to continue increasing its speed has to be checked. Although designed to cruise at Mach 2.2, keeping the speed down to Mach 2 is more economic, exposes the fuselage and airframe to less heating and wear than would occur at the higher speed and thus lengthens the life of the aircraft.

Sitting on the flight deck of any big passenger jet for a landing at London's Heathrow, especially after dark, is always an unnerving experience for the non-pilot. With manual, or pilot-operated landings, there are always a variety of warning horns going off, tripped into action because the aircraft's speed or attitude is becoming less than perfect, but quickly and mysteriously corrected by the pilots. Watching a swan touching down on water helps one to appreciate and understand a Concorde landing. The 'angle of attack' or nose-up attitude is increased to 14°, while the nose itself is lowered, or drooped to its fully-down position of 12.5°. The Flight Engineer, watching his altimeters, calls the height from the runway as it decreases — 'Three hundred, two hundred, one hundred, fifty' — and you seem to be far above it still when the wheels touch with incredible lightness. The nose-up attitude, and the huge swan-like wings have enabled the aircraft to land on a cushion of air trapped beneath the surface of the outspread wings. But touchdown speed is still 170mph, and the dramatic effect of instantly applied reverse thrust makes one thankful for the restraining seat straps.

The glamour of Concorde fades as one enters the airport, to be engulfed in the mass of tired travellers disembarking from the jumbo jets and gathering their wits, children and hand luggage for the slow progress through the immigration lines. Promises in the early years that Concorde passengers would be given priority treatment at this stage proved impossible to fulfil. But even for the most experienced traveller the supersonic journey is something to savour — but not to talk about too much, for fear of irritating one's subsonic friends.

CHAPTER NINE

After Concorde – The Ultimate Aeroplane?

Many doubt whether a successor to Concorde will ever be built — despite the fact that, from the day it went into passenger service, its designers and constructors began studying the parameters of the aeroplane that should come next. It has had many designations — Super Concorde, Concorde Mark Two, Second Generation Concorde, and AST (Advanced Supersonic Transport), among them. The French call it ATSF — Avion de Transport Supersonique Futur. The Americans, as described below, prefer HSCT for High Speed Commercial Transport.

NASA's Director of High Speed Research thinks there will be a US-led successor, and that that will be The Ultimate Aeroplane, because the Earthly globe is just too small to justify anything faster.

Captain Colin Morris, on the flight deck during my London to Washington journey, summed up the situation over his shoulder:

'I would like to see the second generation, 250-seater Mark Two aeroplane, but I don't think we will see it, because the manufacturer has to sell 300, the airlines have to find sufficient routes on which people are prepared to pay premium rates, and it has to be capable of 6,000 miles over the sea or the deserts because we still haven't got over the problem of shock waves, or supersonic bang. Selling 300 aeroplanes and finding enough premium class people to fill them is a tall order.'

That was a good summary of the problems — but much work is being done, and money invested, to produce solutions. In 1989 British Aerospace and Aerospatiale started a five-year study on the feasibility of a successor. By 1992, with two years' research still ahead, it was an eight-party, seven-nation study group, having been joined by Deutsche Aerospace, Boeing, McDonnell Douglas,

147

Alenia, Tupolev and the Japanese aerospace industry. It was led by Bob McKinley, currently Chairman of British Aerospace Airbus Ltd, who was involved as an engineer in the development of Concorde between 1966 and 1979, and then made responsible for supporting Concorde in service and evaluating the possibility of a successor.

In the years since Concorde was designed many advances have been made. New lightweight aluminium alloys and composite metal matrix materials, 'glass cockpit' technology, digital avionics and other weight-saving technologies would enable improvements of around 20% to be made, with matching improvements in the powerplants. British Aerospace's aim in its supersonic studies is an aircraft for 280 passengers in a three-class layout, flying at Mach 2.05 and with a range of 5,500 miles. If there were no fare premium, sales might reach 1500 aircraft, but McKinley's research shows that as higher or premium fares became necessary the market would fall until, if charges were 30% higher, only 400 would be sold.

When the United States abandoned its own planned supersonic aircraft in 1971, at least one billion dollars had been spent on it — about half as much as it cost Britain and France to design, build and fly Concorde. Now millions more are being spent to develop the technologies required to build the 'HSCT', as it is known in Washington. The word 'supersonic' is scrupulously avoided whenever possible, because it tends to arouse bitter political memories.

In a jingoistic speech in December 1992 entitled 'Reclaiming the Wild Blue Yonder', Daniel Goldin, Administrator of the National Aeronautics and Space Administration, called for construction of an all-American HSCT, 'emblazoned with the star spangled banner', which would start carrying passengers in about 2005, with a production line to meet sales of up to 1,000 aircraft providing 140,000 highly-skilled jobs. 'Europe didn't solve the environmental problems when they built the noisy and uneconomical Concorde, but the technological experience they gained allowed them to start Airbus,' he said. (As mentioned earlier in this book, it was the residual facilities, rather than the technological experience, that helped to make Airbus possible.)

Goldin made no mention of US participation in the seven-nation study group which has had the benefit of Anglo-French experience of nearly 25 years of Concorde operations and nearly 150,000hr of supersonic flight. However, there was justification for his approach in that the US continues to spend far more than Europe on the technologies needed for the 21st century's supersonic aircraft.

In 1989 NASA gave contracts worth $284 million to Boeing and McDonnell Douglas to design an HSCT which would have no significant effect on the ozone layer, which would meet the most stringent restrictions on community noise now being imposed on subsonic jets, (technically called FAR 36, Stage Three) and which would produce no perceptible boom over populated areas.

Louis Williams, NASA's Director of High Speed Research, whom I met while in Washington, was more generous when he spoke of Concorde as 'a beautiful airplane and a great technical accomplishment', but which in his view, after two decades of operation still could not be considered an economic success.

Everybody agrees that a successor needs to carry at least twice as many passengers, have a much longer range, making possible transpacific as well as transatlantic flights — and, of course, be environmentally acceptable. So while

148

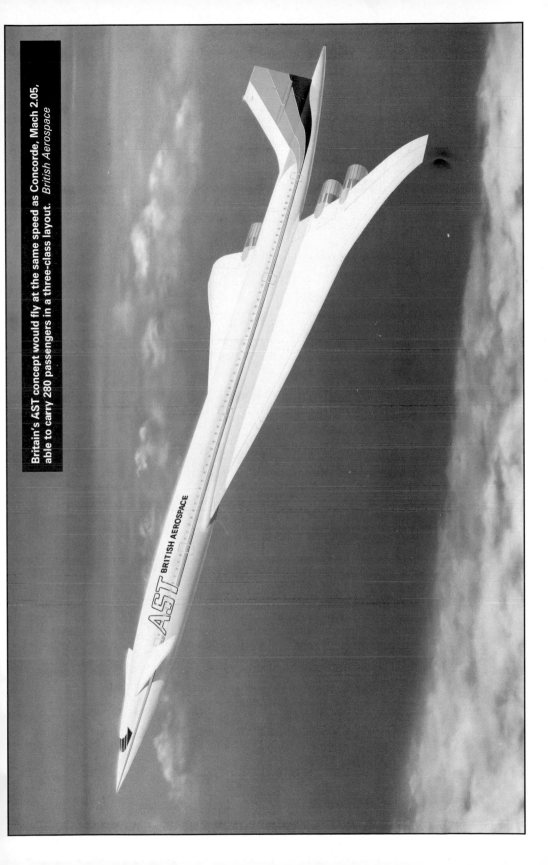

Britain's AST concept would fly at the same speed as Concorde, Mach 2.05, able to carry 280 passengers in a three-class layout. *British Aerospace*

Above: **McDonnell Douglas HSCT concept, flying at Mach 3.2 with 300 passengers, would need to be hydrogen-powered.** *McDonnell Douglas*

Below: **Boeing HSCT concept, twice the size of Concorde, carrying 250 passengers at Mach 2.4 — little faster than Concorde — is regarded as much more feasible and environmentally acceptable.** *Boeing*

Boeing studied a Mach 2.4 concept carrying 250 passengers up to 5,800 miles, McDonnell Douglas was assigned the much more difficult task of studying a Mach 3.2 design able to carry 300 passengers a distance of 7,500 miles. The results, with the benefit of course of later technologies, were a remarkable vindication of the Anglo-French decisions to limit their project to a maximum speed of Mach 2.2. Boeing and McDonnell Douglas found that there was little hope, even with all the new materials available, of designing an aircraft capable of Mach 3 or more, because expensive new fuels such as hydrogen would be required. 'The world is basically too small to justify going faster than Mach 3', Louis Williams told me. 'On a 7,500 mile trip, which is longer than 90% of the routes, today that takes 14 hours. If you travel at Mach 2.2 that takes 6hr, at Mach 4 it's 3.7hr, and then there are very diminishing returns because you are spending all your time accelerating and decelerating.' Adding these factors to the new materials and fuels that would be required to achieve higher speeds, and the need to protect the ozone layer, a speed of Mach 2 to 2.4 made most economic sense.

Since neither company could promise that their designs would be environmentally acceptable, NASA started, in 1989, a new six-year research programme into jet engines capable of providing supersonic flight but making less noise at low level; to 'softening' the supersonic boom by redesigning the fuselage and wings; and to studying the stratosphere to ensure that it would not be damaged by the operations of a large fleet of supersonic aircraft.

Much progress is reported with research on jet engines with 'rich-burn, quick-quench, lean-burn' combustor concepts which would reduce levels of nitrogen oxide formation (the cause, it is thought, of ozone depletion). 'Softening' the boom, so that it would be acceptable at least for flight over lightly populated areas, might be achieved by careful shaping of the aircraft's wing and fuselage, and a technique called 'laminar flow' — upon which Handley Page Aircraft did much pioneering research more than 30 years ago before going bankrupt. Volunteers have been subjected to a wide range of such simulated booms at NASA's Langley Research Center. So far as the stratosphere is concerned, NASA's Upper Atmosphere Research Satellite (UARS), launched by Space Shuttle Discovery in September 1991 and carrying an instrument designed jointly with British scientists, has been busy helping to develop a comprehensive understanding of the potential ozone impact of engine exhaust emissions.

That is being used to supplement information being provided by Nimbus-7, the meteorological satellite which discovered the Antarctic's ozone hole in 1987. A US ozone-mapping spectrometer has been placed aboard a Soviet Meteor-3 satellite; and in 1994 a pilotless aircraft called Perseus, under flight test in California, was due to start measuring ozone depletion with flights above 82,000ft. There is general agreement that future supersonic engines must expel fewer nitrogen oxides, known as NOx, into the upper atmosphere. The amount of pollution produced by an engine per unit of fuel is called the Emission Index, and Concorde's NOx Emission Index is 19 when cruising. A second generation supersonic airliner will have to achieve an Index of only about 5.

British Aerospace's assessments of a Concorde successor are very similar to those of NASA — no doubt at least partly because all the parties to the studies have access to most of the available information. The unanswered questions are: who is to build it, and what will it cost ? There is general reluctance to name a figure, because nearly all the rows over Concorde were due to the way its costs escalated as compared with the original estimates. Bob McKinley estimates that Concorde's costs, escalated from 1975 values to those in 1992, would be between £7 and £8 billion — two or three times the development cost of large subsonic jets. But many technical frontiers were crossed on Concorde which can benefit its successor. McKinley does not say so, but the implication seems to be that development costs might not be much more; and that matches a NASA estimate of $12-15 billion. There is a reasonable market, says McKinley, for one Concorde successor, but not for two or more, so British Aerospace's strategy has been to create an industrial group which would share the costs in return for 'global market access'.

Dan Goldin's nationalistic view of the project is quite different. He wants to walk away from the seven-nation study group and assemble 'Team America' to tackle the project. 'By co-ordinating the passing of the baton between NASA researchers, industry developers, and FAA [Federal Aviation Aministration] certifiers, this is a race in which American can take the gold.' But once NASA has concluded its research, and handed it over — 'passed the baton' — to US industry, it will be for the companies, and principally Boeing and McDonnell Douglas, to decide whether they can raise the money to go ahead on a national basis, or whether to embark on a collaborative project with Europe and/or Japan and Russia.

Bob McKinley calls his briefings and lectures 'Concorde First or Last?' and admits that, balancing the pioneering instincts of an engineer against a business-man's commercial requirements, a decision whether or not to go ahead with a more advanced supersonic airliner is a close-run thing. On balance it should be possible to show that such a project makes technical and commercial sense. And my story ends with his conclusion:

The history of all forms of transport says that the world does not usually go backwards. In the year 2010 grandfathers will not want to say to their grandchildren: 'We used to cross the Atlantic in three and a half hours.'

Appendices

Airline achievement from entry into service, 21 January 1976, to 1 September 1993

	Air France	British Airways	Total
Scheduled passengers	905,316	1,771,700	2,677,016
Charter passengers	136,875*	253,900	390,775
Charter flights	1,998*	3,002	4,963
Flying hours	67,668	105,912	173,580
Supersonic hours	46,014	72,020	118,034
Revenue flights	21,242	33,072	54,314

* to August 1992

Fleet size:
Air France have seven aircraft of which five are operating
British Airways have seven aircraft, all of which are operating

Routes:
Air France
Paris (CDG)-New York (JFK), daily
New York (JFK)-Paris (CDG), daily

British Airways
London (LHR)-New York (JFK), daily
New York (JFK)-London (LHR), daily
London (LHR)-Washington (IAD), 3 times/week
Washington (IAD)-London (LHR), 3 times/week
London-Barbados-London (winter), approx weekly
Various charters

Inaugural passengers aboard London to Washington flight, 25 May 1976

Commercial passengers
A. Allen, President, Cameron Iron Works
D. J. Ashworth, Currys Ltd, competition winner
F. Biggs, Chairman, Biggs Communications Ltd
J. Bintiff
J. Boothroyd
M. C. Brailey, MD, Goode, Durrant & Murray Ltd
Boris Brott, Principal Conductor, BBC Welsh Symphony Orchestra and CBC
    Symphony Orchestra

153

B. Bovey
Mr & Mrs F. Burnett
M. Chaplin
W. Edwards
Mr & Mrs M. A. French, Currys Ltd, competition winners
Mr & Mrs A. Fitzjohn, *Daily Mail*, competition winners
Mr Frank
Ernie Harrison, Chairman, Racal Electronics
Mrs Harrison
A. L. Hunter, Currys Ltd, competition winner
Myron Kahn, President, Polarised Corporation of America
Henry Murray, Director, Arlington Supplies (stamps & Coins) Ltd
Danny O'Donovan, Danny O'Donovan Enterprises
J. Philips
W. Regan
J. Stamper
W. Sterling
K. Telford
John Trotter, Edinburgh bus conductor
Dr & Mrs D. Urquhart
B. Vicars
Mrs M. Wadley
Bernard Winfield, MD, May Winfield & Associates, PR consultants

British Government Representatives
Gerald Kaufman, Minister of State, Dept of Industry
John Tomlinson, Parliamentary Under-Secretary, Foreign Office
Kenneth Binning, Under-Secretary, Concorde Divn, Dept of Industry

Political and Industry Representatives
Julian Amery, MP
Lord Beswick, Chairman, Organising Cttee, British Aerospace
Allen Greenwood, Chairman, BAC
Terrance Higgins, MP
Capt J. C. Kelly-Rogers
Ted Mackenzie, NJC for Civil Air Transport

Media Representatives
James Clark, ABC TV
A/Cdre Teddy Donaldson, *Daily Telegraph*
Michael Donne, *Financial Times*
Christopher English, *Time* magazine
David Fairhall, *The Guardian*
James Godfrey, ABC TV
Wolfgang Helmhold, German Press Agency
John Heasman, ABC TV
Peter Jennings, ABC TV
Miss Lesley Judd, BBC Blue Peter
Angus Macpherson, *Daily Mail*
Patrick Massey, Reuters

Sheldon Meyer, *New York Journal of Commerce*
Ellis Plaice, *Daily Mirror*
Michael Ramsden, *Flight International*
Arthur Reed, *The Times*
Bill Ringle, Gannett Newspapers USA
Frank Robson, *Daily Express*
Ben Shore, Copley News (USA)
Peter Sissons, ITN
Reginald Turnill, BBC TV
Garrick Utley, *Scottish Daily Record*
James Wilkinson, BBC Radio
Derek Wood, *Interavia*
Brian Woosey, *The Sun*

British Airways
Ross Stainton, D/MD & Chief Executive, Overseas Division
Alan Ponsford, Group Public Relations Director
Gordon Davidson, Director Concorde
Capt James Andrew, GM Flight Technical Services

Flight Crew
Capt Brian Calvert, 42, Flight Manager (Technical) Concorde
Capt Norman Todd, 51, Training Manager, Concorde
Flt Eng Lou Bolton, 52

Cabin Crew
Dennis Hill, 45; Frank Heard, 44; John Manhood, 46; Dennis Clacy, 47;Peter Bernard, 38; John Denny,39.

Inaugural Passenger List, London-Bahrain, 21 January 1986

(As issued by BA on that day, provides an insight into the protocol observed on such occassions.)

Fare-Paying

1	Margaret, Duchess of Argyll
2	J. P. Cavanna
3	D. A. Clifton
4	Mrs V. Clifton
5	S. Heaton
6	A. P. Hopkins
7	J. Hurcombe-Blight
8	Viscount Leathers
9	Viscountess Leathers
10	P. Croucher, philatelist with excess baggage
11	John Dorman
12	Deidre Dorman
13	R. J. Pezaro

14	F. E. Jennings
15	E. Thorrsen
16	R. H. Von Gunton
17	Mrs M. Pearce
18	M. Lee
19	Douglas Morrison
20	P. J. Morris
21	Anderson-Wright
22	Mrs E. Patton
23	M. J. Head
24	R. D. Atkin
25	V. C. Buckley
26	P. Cooper
27	R. Ingham
28	Jack LeVian

Non Fare-Paying

29	HRH Duke of Kent
30	Lt Cdr R. Buckley
31	Inspector A. Hawkins
32	Peter Shore, MP, Secretary of State for Trade
33	D. Lee, Parliamentary Private Secretary
34	Eric Varley MP, Secretary of State for Industry
35	J. Michell, Parliamentary Private Secretary
36	David Ennals, MP, Minister for State, Foreign Affairs
37	Kenneth Binning, DG Concorde, Dept of Industry
38	N. Gaffin, Head of Information, Dept of Industry
39	Lord Boyd Carpenter, Chairman, Civil Aviation Authority
40	E. S. Abrahim, Bahrain Embassy, London
41	T. Higgins, MP, Conservative spokesman on trade
42	Russell Kerr, MP, Chairman, Labout Party Aviation Cttee
43	Kenneth Warren, MP, Chairman, Cons Party Aviation Cttee
44	Allen Greenwood, Chairman, BAC.
45	Sir George Edwards, ex-Chairman BAC.
46	Sir Keith Granville, ex-Chairman BOAC.
47	Sir Stanley Hooker, Technical Director, Rolls Royce.
48	N. G. James, BAC, Filton.
49	Gp Capt Leonard Cheshire VC
50	Sir Max Aitken, Chairman, Beaverbrook Newspapers.
51	Thomas Fisher, Chief Executive, Thomas Cook.
52	Captain Brian Trubshaw.
53	Tudor Thomas, D/Gen Sec, Assn of Professional, Executive, Clerical & Computer Staff.
54	Mark Young, Gen Sec, British Airline Pilots Association.

British Airways Staff

55	Henry Marking, D/Chairman & Managing Director, BA.
56	Alan Ponsford, Director of Public Relations.
57	R. Lloyd Davies, BA Engine Overhaul Ltd.

58	E. Wiggins, Avionics Workshop, Overseas Divn.
59	Ross Stainton, D/Man Dir, & Chief Exec, Overseas Divn.
60	Gordon Davidson, Director Concorde, Overseas Divn.
61	Captain J Andrew, GM, Flight Tech Services, Overseas Divn.
63	K. Thorn
64	H. Stewart, Manager, Photographic Services.

Press

65	John Corbett, ITN cameraman (pooled for BBC).
66	Geoffrey Moyse, ITN sound engineer.
67	Walter Moss, ITN sound engineer.
68	Reginald Turnill, BBC Aerospace Correspondent.
69	Peter Sissons, ITN Industrial & Air Correspondent.
70	Patrick Massey, Reuters.
71	Air Cdre Teddy Donaldson, *Daily Telegraph*.
72	Leonard Moxon, Press Association.
73	Arthur Reed, *The Times*.
74	Michael Donne, *Financial Times*.
75	David Fairhall, *The Guardian*.
76	Frank Robson, *Daily Express*.
77	Angus Macpherson, *Daily Mail*.
78	Ellis Plaice, *Daily Mirror*.
79	Brian Woosey, *The Sun*.
80	Michael Ramsden, *Flight International*.
81	James Wilkinson, BBC Radio.
82	Colin Parkes, Independent Radio News.
83	R. Harbour, Australian Associated Press.
84	Gerd Ludemann, Deutsche Press-Agentur.
85	Herman Nicol, *Time* Magazine.
86	Julian Barber, Mutual Radio, USA.
87	Richard Witken, *New York Times*.
88	Jules Bergman, American Broadcasting Company.
89	John Palmer, National Broadcasting Corporation.
90	Chris Callery, NBC cameraman (pooled with ABC).
91	John Hall, NBC sound engineer.
92	John Keeble, *London Evening News*.
93	Roger Bray, *London Evening Standard*.
94	Miss P. Lonnroth, *Stockholm Business Week*.
95	Howard Banks, *The Economist*.
96	Herbert Coleman, *Aviation Week*.
97	Rod Currie, Canadian Press.

Flight Crew
Captain Norman Todd, 51; Captain Brian Calvert, 42; Senior Engineer Officer John Lidiard, 44.

Cabin Crew
Cabin Services Officers John Hawkins, 43; John Hitchcork, 41; Kenneth Taylor, 43; David Brackley, 50; Francine Carville, 38; Sue Graham, 41.

Index

159